THE ALAMO MISSION

FIND THE ANSWERS

How many soldiers were killed in the Battle of the Alamo? (See p. 7.)

How many Spanish missions were founded in Texas? (See p. 8.)

When did San Antonio receive its name? (See p. 18.)

When and where was San Antonio Mission founded? (See pp. 12, 25-26, 99.)

Who was the true founder of San Antonio? (See pp. 12-13.)

How many sites did San Antonio Mission occupy? (See pp. 35-36.)

How long did the sub mission of San Francisco Xavier last? (See pp. 38-41.)

When was the building of the first stone mission church begun? (See pp. 56, 62, 99.)

Was the second stone church ever completed? (See pp. 62, 101.)

Who saved San Antonio from destruction in 1745? (See pp. 59, 99.)

How did La Villita come into existence? (See p. 73.)

What was the principal reason for the mission's decline? (See p. 76.)

When was San Antonio Mission secularized? (See pp. 80-81, 101.)

How did it get the name of the Alamo? (See pp. 84, 98.)

How long was the former mission used as a hospital? (See pp. 85, 101.)

What kind of a plant is the Margil Vine? (See pp. 90-91.)

THE ALAMO MISSION

San Antonio de Valero
1718-1793

By
Marion A. Habig O.F.M.

FRANCISCAN HERALD PRESS
1434 West 51st St. • Chicago, Ill. 60609

The Alamo Mission: San Antonio de Valero, 1718-1793, by Marion A. Habig O.F.M. Copyright © 1977 by Franciscan Herald Press, 1434 West 51st Street, Chicago, Illinois 60609.

Library of Congress Cataloging in Publication Data:

Habig, Marion Alphonse, 1901-
  The Alamo mission.

  Includes bibliographical references.
  1. Alamo. I. Title.
F394.S2H263   976.4'492   77-6661
ISBN 0-8199-0676-X

Nihil Obstat:
  MARK HEGENER O.F.M.
  Censor Deputatus

Imprimatur:
  MSGR. RICHARD A. ROSEMEYER, J.D.
  Vicar General, Archdiocese of Chicago

April 12, 1977

> "The Nihil Obstat and the Imprimatur are official declarations that a book or pamphlet is free of doctrinal error. No implication is contained therein that those who have granted the Nihil Obstat and the Imprimatur agree with the contents, opinions, or statements expressed."

MADE IN THE UNITED STATES OF AMERICA

CONTENTS

Foreword 7
Acknowledgments 9
The Alamo Mission 10
Fr. Antonio Olivares 13
Mission San Francisco Solano 15
The Expedition of 1709 17
Fr. Olivares in Mexico City 20
Waiting for Governor Alarcón 21
Founding of Mission San Antonio 25
Beginning of the Mission 27
Accident of Fr. Olivares 30
Missionaries at San Antonio 32
Second and Third Site of the Mission 35
Mission San Francisco Xavier 38
Aguayo's Offer of Supplies 39
Attempts to Establish the Mission 40
Successors of Fr. Hidalgo 46
Governor Franquis de Lugo 48
The Epidemic of 1739 49
Visit of Fr. Ortiz, 1745 56
The Apache Indians 58
Second Visit of Fr. Ortiz, 1756 62
Report of 1762 64
Zacatecan Friars at San Antonio 70
Fr. Morfi's Account of San Antonio 71
Report of Fr. López, 1789 76
Suppression of the Mission, 1793 80
Inventory of the Mission 81
Subsequent History of the Mission 84
Legend of the Margil Vine 87
Missionaries at the San Antonio Mission 93
Important Dates 99

ILLUSTRATIONS

The Alamo, second stone church of San Antonio
  Mission, 1757 10
Order of the viceroy for the founding of San Antonio 19
One of the bells of San Antonio Mission, 1720 24
The Aguayo Map of San Antonio, 1729 29
Ven. Fr. Antonio Margil, in San Antonio from
  1719 to 1721 31
Plan of the Presidio de San Antonio de Béxar, 1722 34
Plan of Mission San Antonio de Valero, by
  Corner in 1890 37
Acequia and farm of San Antonio Mission 42
Acequia and farm of Purísima Concepción Mission 43
Acequia and farm of San José Mission 44
Acequias and farms of San Juan and Espada Missions 45
Painting by Gentilz of the Alamo (San Antonio
  Mission), ca. 1847 51
Painting by Gentilz of Purísima Concepción Mission 52
Painting by Gentilz of San José Mission 53
Painting by Gentilz of San Juan Capistrano Mission 54
Painting by Gentilz of San Francisco de la Espada Mission 55
Ambulatory of the convento of San Antonio
  Mission (restored) 61
The Alamo (San Antonio Mission church), ca. 1874 69
Plan of Villa de San Fernando (San Antonio), by
  Corner in 1890 74
Corner's key to his plan of Villa de San Fernando 75
Author's plan of Mission San Antonio de Valero 79
Spanish settlements on the San Antonio River,
  late 18th century 92
Facade of the Alamo (church of San Antonio Mission) 100

FOREWORD

MOST Americans know that the Alamo once served as a fort — the fort in which 215 Texans, fighting for independence from Mexico, entrenched themselves and held out to the bitter end in a bloody battle with Santa Anna's army of over 5,000 soldiers. For ten days the Texans held the Mexicans at bay; but on Sunday, March 6, 1836, one hour before dawn, the Mexicans launched a determined assault. Two or three hours later the Battle of the Alamo ended in sudden silence. All of the 183 defenders of the Alamo had been slain. The thirty-two survivors were non-combatants — women, children, and black slaves. The number of Mexican soldiers killed in the battle was 1,544 — almost one-third of Santa Anna's army.

"Remember the Alamo!" became the battle cry in the Texans' war for independence; and six weeks later, on April 21, Sam Houston's forces won the war, after eighteen minutes of actual combat, in the Battle of San Jacinto, by capturing Santa Anna himself.

Not many people are acquainted with the previous history of the Alamo and know that for 75 years during the eighteenth century it was an Indian mission, and that the main building was originally constructed to serve as the church of Mission San Antonio de Valero.

The Alamo has been and should be remembered also as one of the most successful Indian missions among the 36 which were founded in 1632-1793 by the Spanish Franciscan padres within the confines of the present State of Texas — plus one near Nachitoches, Louisiana — and as the first in a chain of five missions established on the banks of the San Antonio River in the present city of San Antonio (1718-1731).

In the pages which follow we offer a short history of the San Antonio de Valero Mission — the Alamo Mission — which deserves to be recalled and remembered along with the later history of the Alamo. It too is an interesting and inspiring story. Basically this little book is a revision and correction of Chapters II and III of the writer's *The Alamo Chain of Missions: A History of San Antonio's Five Old Missions* (Bicentennial Second Edition, Franciscan Herald Press, Chicago, 1976). New facts and information learned by further research during the past decade have been added. Only the principal sources will be cited in the footnotes. For an exhaustive bibliography see *The Alamo Chain of Missions,* pp. 274-293. Copies of most of the primary sources are in the microfilm collection of Old Spanish Missions Historical Research Library at San José Mission in San Antonio (abbreviated RLSJ). — M. A. H.

ACKNOWLEDGMENTS

The photos of the Alamo, by Long, on the front and back cover, and those on pages 3, 69, and 99, were sent to us for this book by Dr. Félix Almaráz of the University of Texas in San Antonio and are used with the permission of the Daughters of the Republic of Texas who are the custodians of the Alamo.

To Dr. Félix Almaráz we are indebted also for the photo of the San Antonio Mission bell, cast in 1720, now in Midland, Texas (p. 24); and it is reproduced by courtesy of Mr. Don Hedgpeth, Director of the Nita Stewart Haley Memorial Library and the J. Evetts Haley History Center in Midland, Texas.

The photo of the ambulatory of the restored section of the friary of San Antonio Mission (now a museum) is by Mr. Miller of *The Washingtonian* (Washington, Mo.) and is a gift from him to the author.

The original of Viceroy Marqués de Valero's order of December 28, 1716, in behalf of Fr. Olivares for the founding of San Antonio (p. 19), is in the Archives of the Franciscan Apostolic College of Santa Cruz de Querétaro, now in Celaya, Mexico; and a copy is in the Old Spanish Missions Historical Research Library at San José Mission in San Antonio.

William Corner's plans (pp. 37, 74, and 75) are from his book, *San Antonio de Béxar: A Guide and History*, published at San Antonio in 1890.

The plan of the mission compound of San Antonio de Valero (p. 79) is a revision of the one in the author's *The Alamo Chain of Missions* (Chicago, 1968, and revised edition 1976). Similarly, the plan of the irrigation ditches and farms of the five San Antonio missions (pp. 42-45) and the Aguayo Map (p. 29) are from his *San Antonio's Mission San José* (Chicago and San Antonio, 1968).

The portrait (engraving) of Ven. Fr. Antonio Margil (p. 31) is taken from Leutenegger-Habig, *Nothingness Itself* (Chicago, 1976).

The second stone church of San Antonio Mission, begun in 1756 or earlier. The year 1757 is inscribed on the façade. This church was never completed during mission days, that is, before the secularization of the mission in 1793.

THE ALAMO MISSION
SAN ANTONIO DE VALERO

THE City of San Antonio in Texas is the site of "the oldest identifiable village within the present limits of the United States." That is the conclusion at which Dr. Robert T. Hill arrived when he traced the route of Cabeza de Vaca and his three companions during their eight-year sojourn and march in Texas, 1528-1536.[1]

The four survivors of the 300 men who took part in the Narváez Expedition of 1527-1528, namely Cabeza de Vaca, Alonso del Castillo, Andrés Dorantes, and Estevanico the Moor, after being held captives by Indians of Texas for seven years, regained their freedom in October, 1535, and headed for Mexico. In June, 1536, they arrived at a friendly Indian rancho or village which was situated near San Pedro Springs on the banks of the San Antonio River; and from there they continued westward toward Del Rio and Mexico. That is one opinion, at least. Different scholars have identified the places mentioned by Cabeza in a different way.

There is no doubt, however, that the expedition of the first Spanish governor of Texas, Domingo Terán de los Ríos, and the Franciscan missionary Fr. Damian Massanet (Mazanet),

---
1. The Dallas *News*, November 11, 1933.

while on their way to eastern Texas in 1691, visited an Indian village called Yanaguana on the banks of the San Antonio River. It was the 13th of June, the feast day of Saint Anthony of Padua, the universally popular saint and wonder-worker of the thirteenth-century and an early follower of St. Francis of Assisi. For this reason Fr. Massanet gave the name of San Antonio to Yanaguana, and the governor named the river the Rio de San Antonio. This place, they noted, was an ideal spot for a future mission and settlement.[2]

The mission and settlement of San Antonio, however, were founded only after the first missions in eastern Texas had failed and new ones were founded in 1716. There is a persistent ancient tradition that already in 1715-1716 a few Spaniards from San Juan Bautista on the Rio Grande established an unauthorized settlement below San Pedro Springs "in the present Ruiz-Arbor Place in San Antonio."[3] But there is no convincing evidence to support the tradition.

The City of San Antonio definitely had its beginning when the Mission of San Antonio de Valero was begun on the west bank of the San Antonio River near San Pedro Springs on May 1, 1718, and four days later the Presidio and Villa of San Antonio de Béxar were formally established.

Officially, the founder was Don Martin de Alarcón, Governor of Coahuila and "Governor of Texas and such other lands as might be conquered." But he merely carried out the instructions he received from the viceroy of New Spain; and he did so only after a delay of an entire year.

The true founder, not only of the mission but also of the presidio and villa, was a Franciscan missionary of the College of Querétaro, Fr. Antonio de San Buenaventura y Olivares. Dr. Castañeda wrote of him that "he may justly be called the true father of the idea," that is, "of the founding of a mission

---

2. M. A. Habig, *The Alamo Chain of Missions: A History of San Antonio's Five Old Missions,* revised edn. (Chicago, 1976), pp. 160-162.
3. Ben Cuellar Ximenes, *Gallant Outcasts* (San Antonio, 1963), p. 164.

and the establishment of the nucleus for a civil government on the San Antonio River. It was he and no other who conceived the plan, succeeded in winning the approval of the viceroy, and was instrumental in obtaining the final authorization of the project. Ever since 1709, he had longed for an opportunity to put his plan into execution."[4] We may add that it was ever since 1700.

Fr. Antonio Olivares

Before he joined the College of Querétaro, which was founded in 1683, Fr. Olivares had been a missionary of the Franciscan Province of Zacatecas for many years. Although advanced in years, he was sent in 1699 to the Mission of San Juan Bautista, recently founded in Coahuila, north of present Sabinas, Mexico. For reasons beyond his control, he was forced to abandon the mission soon afterwards and to retire with his companion to Mission Nuestra Señora de los Dolores, near present Lampazos.

Nothing daunted, Fr. Olivares then undertook the establistment of another Mission San Juan Bautista on the west side of the Rio Grande, not far from Eagle Pass, Texas. With two companions he arrived at this place on January 1, 1700, and named it the Valle de Circuncisión. After founding the new mission with more than five hundred Indians of the same

---
4. C. E. Castañeda, *Our Catholic Heritage in Texas*, 7 vols. (Austin, 1936-1958), II, 78.

tribes as those who had been gathered on the Sabinas, Fr. Olivares left it in the care of his companions and made an expedition into the present state of Texas. Incidentally most historians fail to mention this expedition among those made into Texas in the early eighteenth century.[5]

Accompanied by Captain José de Urrutia and a few soldiers, Fr. Olivares traveled some thirty leagues (75 miles) after crossing the Rio Grande and went as far as the Rio Frio. Here and on the way he found numerous friendly and docile Indians who were willing and anxious to settle down in one or more missions. Fr. Olivares would have liked to remain on the Rio Frio, but the distance from San Juan Bautista was too great. With the firm hope and intention of establishing new missions in this part of Texas later on, he returned to the Rio Grande.

At this time Bishop Felipe Chaves Galindo of Guadalajara was visiting the establishments in Coahuila; and Fr. Olivares personally made a report to him about his trip into Texas and the prospects of new missions in that area. On Easter Day, 1701, the bishop convoked a meeting of the missionaries and officials of Coahuila; and it was decided that a presidio and additional missions should be established near San Juan Bautista Mission as a stepping stone for new missions beyond the Rio Grande.

The bishop prepared a memorial in which he requested the viceroy, Don José Sarmiento de Valladares, Conde de Moctezuma, to establish a presidio on the Rio Grande; and Fr. Olivares was chosen to go to Mexico City in order to present the matter to the viceroy. He succeeded in obtaining the necessary approval; and the Presidio of San Juan Bautista was established near the mission of the same name. In accordance with the viceroy's orders, the presidios of Nueva Vizcaya and Coahuila provided a total of thirty soldiers for the new presidio;

---

5. Fr. Isidro Felix de Espinosa, *Crónica de los Colegios de Propaganda Fide de la Nueva España*, New Edition with Notes and Introduction by Lino G. Canedo (Washington, 1964), pp. 754-755.

and these were placed under the command of Captain Diego Ramón.[6]

Returning from Mexico City, Fr. Olivares stopped at Querétaro, where Fr. Francisco Hidalgo was then the Fr. Guardian of the College. With two new missionaries, he went back to Mission San Juan Bautista and Mission San Francisco Solano nearby. A third mission, San Bernardo (of which the ruins are still standing) was founded in the vicinity early in 1702. For the latter the Duquesa de Sessa, wife of the viceroy, donated the church furnishings. For Mission San Francisco Solano Fr. Olivares had also brought along such furnishings from Mexico City.

Mission San Francisco Solano

With the founding of San Francisco Solano, which had taken place as early as March 1, 1700, Mission San Antonio de Valero may be said to have had its beginning. For it was this mission which was later transferred to the San Antonio River.

At San Francisco Solano and the other two missions, churches of adobe with adjoining residences for the padres, were constructed; irrigation ditches were dug; and farms were cultivated. In a short time, Fr. Olivares gathered at his mission more than three hundred Indians, not counting little children, namely Jarames, Siabanes, and Payoguanes. In the morning

---

6. *Ibid.,* pp. 755-757.

and in the evening, he instructed them in Christian doctrine; and soon he was able to baptize more than 150 of them.

All three missions prospered to such an extent that it was found they were too close together. In 1703, therefore, Fr. Olivares moved San Francisco Solano to the Valle de San Ildefonso, sixteen leagues (forty miles) west of San Juan Bautista. Only a few Jarames went along to the new site; but about four hundred Indians of various tribes were quickly assembled, and success crowned the efforts of Fr. Olivares during the next three years.

In 1706 Fr. Olivares was elected Fr. Guardian of the College for a term of three years. Two years later, young Fr. Isidro Félix de Espinosa reported to him that 140 Indian families (about 420 persons) were living at Mission San Juan Bautista, 200 families (about 600 persons) at San Bernardo, and about 400 Indians at San Francisco Solano. But later that year, all the mission Indians except a few Jarames fled into the mountains because of the nearness of the barbarous and cruel Tobosos. Not long afterwards eight Jarames were killed five miles from the mission.

The furnishings of the church were then taken to San Juan Bautista for safekeeping, but the mission was not abandoned entirely. A Franciscan brother of the Third Order of St. Francis remained with a few Jarames for an entire year, instructed them morning and evening, and helped them to maintain the farm. On feast days a missionary from San Juan Bautista traveled to San Francisco Solano to celebrate holy Mass and to baptize the sick and the children. He made the trip of eighty miles in twenty-four hours, because his services were needed on the Rio Grande, where the missionaries had the spiritual care also of the presidio.

A new missionary from Querétaro was then assigned to San Francisco Solano; but all his efforts to restore the mission to its former status failed, and it was moved once more back to the Rio Grande to a place called San José. This was three leagues (seven and a half miles) distant from the other two missions. An adobe church was built and some of the fugitive Indians came back, since they had the protection of the nearby presidio.

The Expedition of 1709

Ever since 1693, when the first two missions which had been founded in eastern Texas had to be abandoned, one of the missionaries who had taken part in the venture, Fr. Francisco Hidalgo, while continuing his work in Coahuila and serving as guardian of the College (1701-1703), had persistently advocated by every means at his disposal the re-establishment of missions among the friendly Tejas and the permanent occupation of the Province of Texas.

During the last year of his term as guardian at the College (1709), Fr. Olivares was informed by Fr. Espinosa about a report that the Tejas or some of them had moved to the Colorado River, which was much closer to the Rio Grande. Fr. Olivares not only agreed that it was worthwhile to investigate the correctness of the report but joined Fr. Espinosa and Captain Pedro de Aguirre of the San Juan Bautista Presidio in an expedition to the Colorado.

From the diary which Fr. Espinosa[7] kept during this expedition we learn that the report rested only on the fact that the Tejas sometimes wandered as far as the Colorado on their buffalo hunts. On the way, however, the party crossed the San Antonio River near San Pedro Springs, and found it an ideal spot for a Spanish settlement and mission.

Unaware of the fact that in 1691 Fr. Damian Massanet and Domingo Terán de los Ríos had already given the name of San Antonio to the river and to an Indian village which they found on its banks, Frs. Olivares and Espinosa, by a happy coincidence, likewise named the river the Rio de San Antonio.

More important, however, was Fr. Olivares' decision that not only should the missions among the Tejas be re-established, but one or more missions should be founded also on the Rio de San Antonio near the springs. This center would serve as a halfway station between San Juan Bautista and eastern Texas as well as the headquarters for missionary work among the other Indians of Texas, including those he had encountered near the Rio Frio in 1700.

After completing his term as guardian in 1709, Fr. Olivares was sent to Spain to recruit new missionaries for Texas. After his return, he resumed his work at Mission San Francisco Solano, and looked forward to the day when his plans for Texas could be realized.

---

7. Fr. Espinosa's Diary of 1709, trans. by Gabriel Tous in *The Espinosa-Olivares-Aguirre Expedition of 1709* (*Texas Catholic Historical Society Preliminary Studies*, I, no. 3, Austin, 1930).

Don Balthasar de Zuñiga y Guzman Soto
mayor de Mendoza Marques de Valero, Ayamonte
y Alenquer, Gentil hombre de Camara de su Mag.d
de su Cons.o Camara y Junta de Guerra de Yndias
Virrey Gov.or y Cap.n Gen.l destta Nueva Sp.a
y Presidente de la R.l aud.a della &c.=
Resuelto que el Padre fr. Antonio de San
Buenaventura Olivares del orden de San fran.co
Misionero Apostolico del Colleg.o de la Santa Cruz
de Queretaro, pase a Poblar en la Prov.a de los texas la Mision de S.n Antonio y siendo Precizo q.e
assi su Persona como la de sus Comp.ros Religiosos y
demas que fueren en el, y tambien lo que lleva ca-
targa referida Mision baia con el Resguardo q.e se
Requiere, por el Presente atendiendo a lo q.e esto
he cito en Consulto y en conformd. de mi Decreto
de o. dia de la fha. Mando a todos los Gover-
nadores Alcaldes m.res y Cap.nes de los Presidios
por donde Pasare el R.P. que conduze a todas
las Conveniencias para d.ha Mision Como son, or-
nam.tos adornos de Yglesia ageros para labrar
y Repartirlas el Regalo a los Yndios de

Fr. Olivares in Mexico City

When six missions were finally established in eastern Texas in 1716 and 1717, with the cooperation of the College of Nuestra Señora de Guadalupe de Zacatecas, Fr. Olivares did not go along. Instead he was sent again to Mexico City to obtain from the viceroy fuller governmental support for the new missions in eastern Texas and to propose his own plan for a mission, presidio, and settlement on the Rio de San Antonio.

Fr. Olivares arrived in the capital late in September, 1716, and remained until December 28. He had a conference with the new viceroy, the Marqués de Valero, Don Baltazar de Zúñiga, and presented two written memorials. The first was concerning eastern Texas. In the second, dated November 20, he proposed to move his Mission of San Francisco Solano from the west side of the Rio Grande to the Rio de San Antonio. There were only a few Christian Jarame Indians at San Francisco Solano, but these would be very helpful as teachers of the pagan Indians who would be congregated at the new site. He envisioned the latter as numbering from three to four thousand. He asked for a guard of ten soldiers until the Indians had been assembled on the San Antonio River; and he suggested that civilans of Mexico be induced to form a settlement near the mission by offering them free land and water rights.

After consulting his advisors, the viceroy gave his approval to all of Fr. Olivares' requests; and on December 7, he appointed Don Martín de Alarcón (who was already governor of Coahuila since August 5) governor also of Texas, for the purpose of bringing aid to the missions of eastern Texas and of helping Fr. Olivares to establish the mission on the San Antonio, near which he was to found a presidio and a settlement.

On December 28, after receiving a favorable order from the viceroy, Fr. Olivares left for Querétaro, where he selected two companions, Fr. Francisco Ruiz and Brother Pedro Maleta, who were to assist him at the new Mission of San

Antonio. Leaving Querétaro with them on February 9, 1717, he reached Saltillo on March 24; but Governor Alarcón was still in Mexico City and did not arrive at his capital until June. Fr. Olivares went on to Monterrey, and from there to San Juan Bautista, which he reached on May 3.

Waiting for Governor Alarcón

Governor Alarcón was taking his time; but there was no need for Fr. Olivares to wait for him as long as he received the escort and guard of ten soldiers, which the viceroy had granted him. He asked the captains of the presidios of San Juan Bautista and of Coahuila for ten soldiers, but both refused to supply the men.

Fr. Olivares' long disappointing wait had begun; and he did his waiting at Mission San Francisco Solano, which was to be transferred to the Rio de San Antonio. He had to wait almost a full year. Who could remain patient that long? And there were other disappointments besides that of waiting. It was a sore trial for Fr. Olivares, who was a veteran missionary, far advanced in age; and during this period of waiting, his companion Fr. Francisco Ruiz died. Only Brother Pedro Maleta remained to help him establish the new mission.

On June 5, 1717, Fr. Olivares wrote a letter to Alarcón. The governor found it waiting for him when he arrived in Saltillo. In it Fr. Olivares told him about the refusal of the presidio captains to supply ten soldiers; but Alarcón did not reply.

After the governor came to San Juan Bautista on August 3, he assigned eight soldiers to Fr. Olivares at Mission San Francisco Solano to guard the supplies the missionary had gathered; but they were careless guards and had instructions to take orders only from the governor, not the missionary.

As many as 150 Indians from the San Antonio area came to visit Fr. Olivares. Would a mission really be established on the Rio de San Antonio? Why the delay? They were anxious to settle down at the new mission.

About the middle of September, Fr. Olivares wrote a letter to Alarcón, and begged him to furnish the ten soldiers so he could go on alone. But the governor replied that he could not spare the men. It would have been foolhardy to try to make the transfer from Mission San Francisco Solano to the new mission on the San Antonio without the military escort; and so Fr. Olivares had to keep on waiting — waiting until the spring of the following year.[8]

Finally on February 16, 1718, Alarcón and his party of 72 persons, including three missionaries and the soldiers (of whom six, according to Fr. Pérez de Mesquía, took along their families), crossed the Rio Grande and then stopped there for another seven weeks. Fr. Olivares was not among the missionaries. The eight guards assigned to his mission would now have to serve as an escort anyway; and Fr. Olivares preferred to make the journey to the San Antonio River independently of Alarcón's expedition.

The missionaries with Alarcón were: Fr. Pedro Pérez de Mesquía, who had been a missionary in Coahuila and later (1724-1727) was the guardian of the College of Querétaro: Fr. Joseph Guerra, a member of the College of Querétaro;[9] and Fr. Francisco Céliz, a missionary in Coahuila belonging to the

---

8. Castañeda, *op. cit.,* II, 79-91.
9. This Fr. José Guerra, a member of the College of Querétaro, must be distinguished from the one (same name) who succeeded Fr. Antonio Margil as the Fr. Guardian of the College of Zacatecas, 1713-1717. Cf. B. Leutenegger and M. A. Habig, *The Zacatecan Missionaries in Texas, 1716-1834* (Texas Historical Survey Committee, Report No. 23, Austin, 1973), p. 131.

Franciscan Province of Zacatecas, serving as the official chaplain and diarist of Alarcón's expedition. Fr. Pérez de Mesquía also kept a short diary.[10]

On April 9 (the 7th says Fr. Pérez de Mesquía) Alarcón's party finally got under way. Besides a herd of cattle, they were taking along 548 horses, of whom 300 as well as most of the cattle had been furnished by the Marqués de Aguayo from his huge ranch in Coahuila.

On April 15, special instructions from the viceroy were delivered to Alarcón. The latter misinterpreted them and changed the direction of his march toward Lavaca Bay until the 23rd, when he reversed his decision and headed for San Pedro Springs and the San Antonio River, arriving there on the 25th.

Fr. Pérez de Mesquía says the water of the springs was sweet and this place was very pleasant because of the trees surrounding it. The volume of the water at the point where the flow from the two springs met to form San Pedro Creek was five and a half feet wide and four feet deep; and though the stream had a swift current, the water could easily be led off to irrigate "good and sufficient lands."

---

10. Fr. Pedro Pérez de Mesquía's Diary, "Mesquía Diary of the Alarcón Expedition into Texas, 1718," trans. by Fritz Leo Hoffman, in *Southwestern Historical Quarterly,* vol. 41 (Jan., 1938).

One of the four bells which were at San Antonio Mission in 1745. This bell, cast in 1720, is now in Midland, Texas. Another, cast in 1749, is in the museum at the restored Presidio od La Bahía near Goliad; it has a long crack and a bullet hole. A bell, weighing 150 pounds, was brought to Texas in 1690 for the San Francisco Mission, founded that year in eastern Texas. Buried when this mission had to be abandoned in 1693, it was recovered by Governor Alarcón in the fall of 1718 and taken by him to San Antonio.

Founding of Mission San Antonio

For some reason or other, Fr. Olivares and Brother Maleta with their escort of soldiers and some Jarame Indians did not leave the former San Francisco Solano Mission until April 18; but they probably covered the distance to San Antonio in half the time that it took Alarcón and thus arrived about the same time as the governor's party.

Anyhow, Fr. Olivares immediately constructed a temporary mission chapel with the aid of three Jarame Indians. Fr. Pérez de Mesquía says it was about a mile south of San Pedro Springs, on high ground, near a small grove of oak trees, where they found Fr. Olivares building a hut for himself. Fr. Céliz writes that the site which Fr. Olivares picked for his mission was almost two miles south of the springs, along San Pedro Creek, on the west side of San Antonio River.

Dr. Castañeda remarks that, "since the mission stayed at its first location, the chronicler meant river where he says creek."[11] However, we have the testimony of Fr. Isidro Felix de Espinosa confirming that of Frs. Pérez de Mesquía and Céliz. The first location of the mission, he writes, was on the west bank of the San Antonio River, and only after about a year did Fr. Olivares transfer it to the east side, where the land was better and it could be more easily irrigated.

The formal founding of Mission San Antonio de Valero by Governor Alarcón, with the usual ceremonies, did not take place until May 1; and four days later, the governor officially established the Presidio of San Antonio de Béxar and the Villa de Béxar near San Pedro Springs. According to the governor's own statement, the Villa comprised only ten families, and twenty more came to San Antonio later. In 1722 the Marqués de Aguayo moved the presidio and villa to the west side of the San Antonio River, 200 *varas* (about 550 feet) from the bank, opposite the mission which was then on the east side.

---

11. Castañeda, *op. cit.*, II, 92, is mistaken when he writes: ". . . the mission stayed at its first location."

Among those who were present at the founding of Mission San Antonio was Fr. Miguel Núñez de Haro, later one of the first two missionaries of Mission San José y San Miguel de Aguayo. Because of the dilatory ways of Alarcón, the missions in eastern Texas were in dire straits by the end of 1717. Only then was Fr. Núñez commissioned to take a train of supplies with an escort of soldiers to eastern Texas from San Juan Bautista. When they reached the Trinity, it had overflowed its banks and looked like the sea. It was impossible to cross the river. At the cost of great hardships, Fr. Núñez waited for two months, then hid the supplies, and gave a letter to a Tejas Indian for the missionaries in eastern Texas. On the return trip Fr. Núñez met Alarcón west of the Medina on April 21, and went along to San Antonio. He administered the first baptism at the new mission to a dying child on the day of its founding, May 1.

"Valero" was added to the name of the mission, because the Marquis de Valero was the viceroy of New Spain at the time; and "Béxar" honored the memory of the viceroy's brother, one of Spain's heroes, the Duke of Béxar, who died in the defense of Budapest against the Turks.

In June, 1718, says Fr. Olivares, there were six missionaries at the San Antonio Mission. They were, besides Fr. Olivares himself and Brother Maleta, Fr. Núñez and the three priests who had come with Alarcón, Frs. Pérez de Mesquía, Guerra, and Céliz.

Another missionary passed through San Antonio during the first part of July. He was Fr. Pedro Múñoz, the president or superior of the missions at San Juan Bautista. He had left the latter place on June 27, and on July 21 arrived with a new train of supplies at the place where Fr. Núñez had hid his. Not only did he find the latter intact, but he also met Fr. Espinosa and Captain Ramón who had come to fetch them. The letter which Fr. Núñez had given to the Tejas Indian had finally been delivered.

Fr. Espinosa, who was the president of the three Querétaran missions in eastern Texas, and Captain Ramón, learning that Mission San Antonio and the Villa de Béxar had been established, went to the new foundation to welcome Governor Alarcón, and arrived August 27. With them came the chiefs of 23 tribes who had been in revolt, but now offered their allegiance to the new governor.

Beginning of the Mission

At Mission San Antonio, however, the Indians who had been so desirous to have a mission were slow in coming. In fact, they had suddenly become hostile. In a letter which he wrote to the viceroy on June 22, 1718, Fr. Olivares mentioned the fact that Alarcón had treated his Indian guide so badly that the latter ran away after they reached San Antonio and joined the Indians of the vicinity; and Alarcón had made the threat that if the Indians would not come to the mission, he would go in search of them and put them to the sword. That was no doubt one reason why the Indians did not come.

Accompanied by 29 persons, including Frs. Espinosa, Guerra, and Céliz, Alarcón made a side trip to Lavaca Bay in September, 1718. Returning to San Antonio, he finally set out for eastern Texas on September 28. Fr. Núñez may have gone along with the others. At any rate, Fr. Olivares was now the only priest in San Antonio. But, with the help of Brother Maleta and his Jarame friends, he was able to gather a large number of Payaya and Pamaya Indians at Mission San Antonio de Valero during the months that followed.

When Alarcón returned on January 12, 1719, to San Antonio from eastern Texas, without having accomplished anything worthwhile there to the missionaries' great disappointment, he found numerous Indians at Fr. Olivares' mission, gave them gifts, and appointed Indian officials for the pueblo. He was edified on seeing the Indians assemble for prayer when the mission bell was rung. He had brought along a bell that he had found on the site of the first mission of San Francisco which had been abandoned in 1693. It weighed six *arrobas* (about 150 pounds). The entire month of January was spent in digging irrigation ditches for the presidio and villa and for the mission.

Although Mission San Antonio and a little presidio and villa were established, the Alarcón expedition, expensive though it was, had accomplished little; and not only Fr. Olivares but also the other missionaries were altogether dissatisfied with the governor. Returning to Saltillo, Alarcón asked the viceroy for more soldiers; and when his request was not granted he tendered his resignation early in 1719. The viceroy accepted it immediately, but Alarcón continued in office until the end of the year.[12]

---

12. *Ibid.*, II, 102-109.

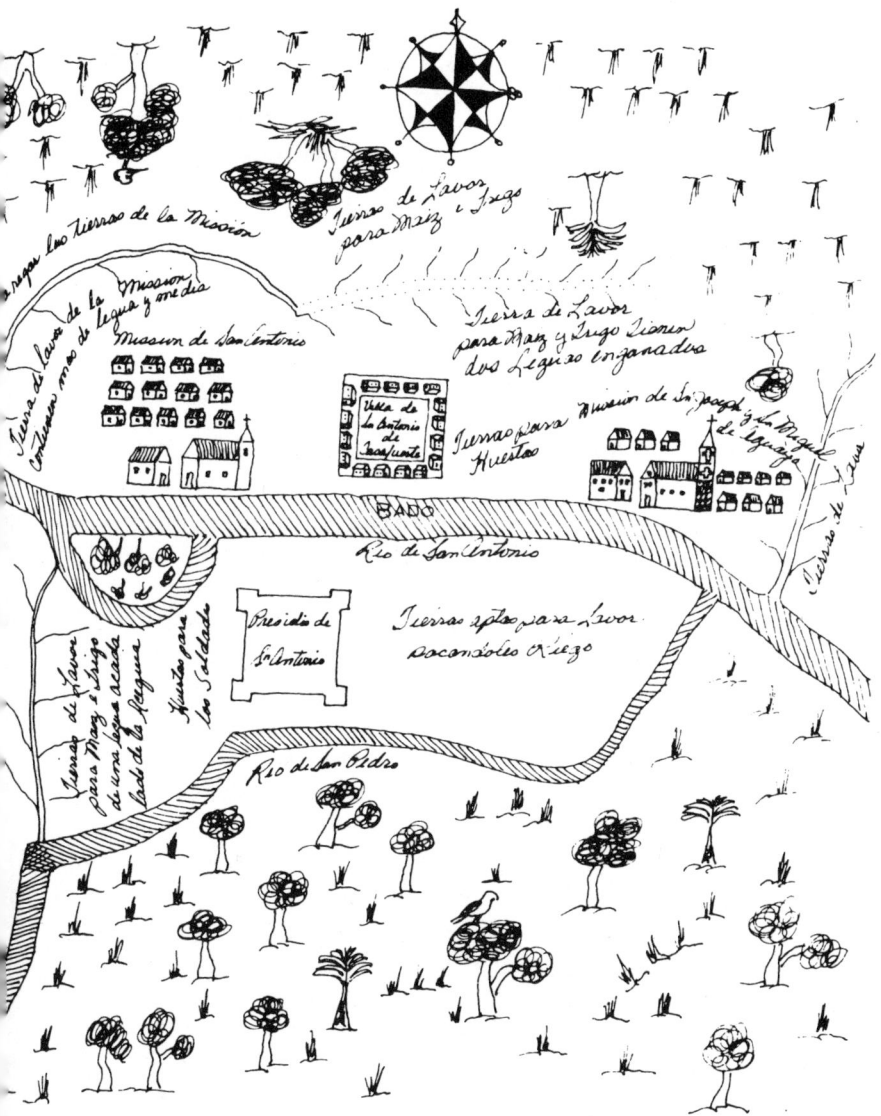

of San Antonio drawn by or for the Marqués de Aguayo in 1729, seven years after he had n there. At the time, he recommended the establishment of a villa of Canary Islanders lla de Casafuerte) on the east side of the San Antonio River; it became the Villa de San nando on the west side of the river in 1731. The map places the loop of the river on the ong side; and the juncture of San Pedro Creek with the river is farther north. San José sion, founded on the east side in 1720, was moved before 1727 to its second site on the t side close to the river bank, and after 1739 to its third and present site.

Accident of Fr. Olivares

It must have been in the spring of 1719 that Fr. Olivares had a serious accident. Fr. Espinosa tells us about it in his *Crónica,* which was printed in 1746-1747. "At the mission's first location," he writes, "Fr. Olivares maintained himself for more than a year; and in the beginning he did not have a priest companion, because the one who had been assigned to him died before his departure from the Rio Grande. During this time, he suffered an accident as he passed over a wooden bridge, covered with earth, which was near the mission. The beast on which he was riding broke through with one leg; and the blow that the father received as he fell was such that it broke one of his legs.

"This put him in the greatest danger, and it was necessary to send a messenger to the missions on the Rio Grande to get a confessor. Riding on a beast, Fr. Pedro Múñoz came immediately and with such speed that in forty continuous hours he covered the eighty leagues (about 200 miles) which, according to the soldiers, is the distance from the Rio Grande to San Antonio. The presence of a priest at his side gave mucn consolation to the sick man; and after he had made his confession he could give greater attention to the care of his leg.

"The Lord was kind to him and enabled one of the soldiers to promote the knitting of the broken bone by the application of home remedies. The father had to remain in bed for a long time, but in the end the leg was entirely healed. After he had fully recovered, the father moved the mission to the other side of the San Antonio River, because it offered greater advantages. There the mission has continued down to the present day and enjoyed much success."[13]

---

13. Espinosa, *Crónica,* pp. 735-736.

Ven. Fr. Antonio Margil. Driven from eastern Texas by the French in 1719, he resided at San Antonio Mission till 1721 when Aguayo restored the east-Texas missions.

Missionaries at San Antonio

The transfer of the mission to the east side of the river probably took place in June or July, 1719. At that time Fr. Pedro Múñoz paid another visit to Fr. Olivares, and brought along an assistant in the person of Father Joseph Andrés Rodríguez de Jesús María. These two, at any rate, made no less than twenty-one entries in San Antonio's register of baptisms at the end of June and the early part of July. There is also one entry by Fr. Olivares, for June 28, showing that he had recuperated by that time. There are thirty-six entries by Fr. Rodríguez also in 1720, indicating that this missionary remained with Fr. Olivares.

Mission San Antonio soon proved its worth as a halfway station. In October-November, 1719, the missionaries, soldiers, and settlers of eastern Texas came to San Antonio as refugees. France and Spain were at war, and the French in the colonies learned about it before the Spaniards. The French of Natchitoches had seized the Mission of San Miguel and were on the point of taking the other five as well.

The two Fr. Presidents, Espinosa and Margil, wanted to stay, but the others all thought it best to retreat; and so they too were forced to abandon the missions temporarily. The refugees remained in San Antonio until 1721, when the Marqués de Aguayo and his army of 500 came and re-established the presidio and six missions in eastern Texas and added another presidio at San Miguel de los Adaes.

During the year 1720 there was no lack of assistants, Zacatecan as well as Querétaran, at Mission San Antonio; but the aged founder had now accomplished his great task — the establishment of this mission on a firm basis. The Fr. Guardian of the College of Querétaro decided that it was time for Fr. Olivares to retire to the College for a well deserved rest.

In the register of baptisms of San Antonio Mission[14] we read that on September 8, 1720, by order of the Fr. Guardian Diego de Alcántara, Fr. Olivares turned over the mission to his successor, Fr. Francisco Hidalgo, one of the refugees from eastern Texas. Fr. Olivares went back to Querétaro; and two years later, on June 7, 1722, he died at the College.

Assisted by Fr. Joseph González, Fr. Hidalgo remained in charge of Mission San Antonio for about four years. He welcomed the Marqués de Aguayo when he arrived in San Antonio in 1721 and paid a visit to the mission on April 26. Aguayo found no less than 240 Indians, young and old, residing at the mission; and to all of them he distributed "clothing and other articles which they value highly."

Fr. Hidalgo went back to Mission San Juan Bautista on the Rio Grande in 1724 or later, and there he died November 6, 1726, at the age of 67. To him and to Fr. Olivares must be given the credit, in great measure, for the permanent occupation of the Spanish Province of Texas during the years from 1716 to 1722.

---

14. *Libros de Bautismos, 1703-1783* of Mission San Antonio de Valero in the Archives of the Cathedral of San Fernando, San Antonio. Only eight baptisms are recorded for the years 1703-1718, that is, for the Mission of San Francisco Solano near San Juan Bautista on the Rio Grande. The *Libro 4° de Baptismos* (sic) begins with January 1, 1826, and is continued until March 3, 1858, the last entry having the number 3,716. No entries were made between 1835 and 1840, when Bishop Odin installed Father Miguel Calvo as pastor of San Fernando and the churches of the former missions in the San Antonio area.

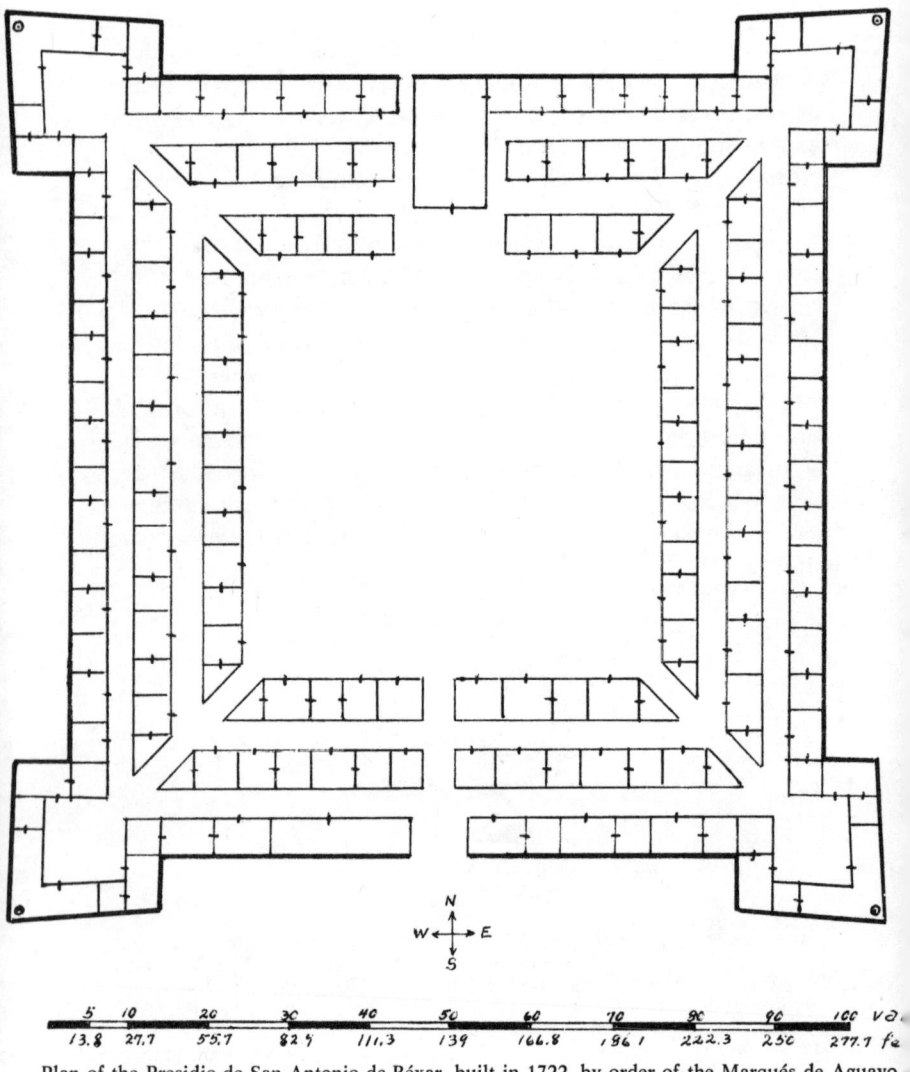

Plan of the Presidio de San Antonio de Béxar, built in 1722, by order of the Marqués de Aguayo.

Second and Third Site of the Mission

When Fr. Olivares moved Mission San Antonio from the west bank of the river to its east bank in the summer of 1719, he did not establish it at its present site. The mission was moved once more some year later to the place it now occupies, namely Alamo Plaza. That much is certain. In his report of 1756, Fr. Ortiz tells us that in the time of Fr. Margil (who was at the mission in 1719-1721) Mission San Antonio was situated "a distancia de mas de una quadra de la Mision" (at a distance of more than a block from the mission's site in 1756).

Charles Ramsdell, who has identified the first site of Mission San Antonio as having been near the present-day Chapel of the Miracles (at the corner of Ruiz and Laredo streets), also tells us that "the second location was very near today's Alamo, about where the Alamo Ditch would cross East Commerce Street, where the Alameda, the avenue lined with cottonwoods, would be laid out in 1805, and where St. Joseph's Church stands."[15]

The transfer from the second to the third and present site (the Alamo Plaza) was made in 1724 after a hurricane struck the mission which at that time consisted of fragile huts and a small stone chapel with a tower. This we learn from the report of an official visit or inspection of the mission made by Fr. Miguel Sevillano de Paredes in November, 1727. At this time, San Antonio Mission was still included among the so-called San Juan Bautista or Rio Grande missions; and the Fr. President of the latter was also the superior of the missionaries in San Antonio.

Fr. Sevillano's report shows that in 1727 San Antonio Mission, which began with five Indians in 1718, had a total of 60 resident Indian families or 273 persons. The structures were still temporary *jacales*, but the stone for a church had been

---

15. C. Ramsdell, *San Antonio: A Historical and Pictorial Guide* (Austin, 1959), pp. 16-17.

gathered. It had been necessary to dig an *acequia* or irrigation ditch and to till the fields before more permanent buildings could be constructed.[16]

The opinion that the third site of San Antonio Mission was an intermediate spot between St. Joseph Church and the Alamo Plaza and that the latter was the fourth site[17] (at the San Antonio River) is based on the use of the words "two gun shots" as being the distance from the Presidio de San Antonio de Béxar on the west side of the river. This opinion cannot be correct, since the later reports of 1745, 1762, and 1777, speaking of the third and final site of Mission San Antonio, all use the same expression, "a distance of two gun shots," to indicate how far the mission was from the Villa de San Fernando and its church (or the nearby Presidio).

---

16. Fr. Miguel Sevillano de Paredes, "Visita de las Misiones del Rio Grande, 1727," in Archivo General y Publico de la Nación, Mexico City, Historia, vol. 29, pp. 35-41; cf. R. S. Weddle, *San Juan Bautista: Gateway to Spanish Texas* (Austin, 1968), pp. 17, 185.

17. Lon Tinkle, "The Alamo," in *Six Missions of Texas* (Waco, 1965), p. 9.

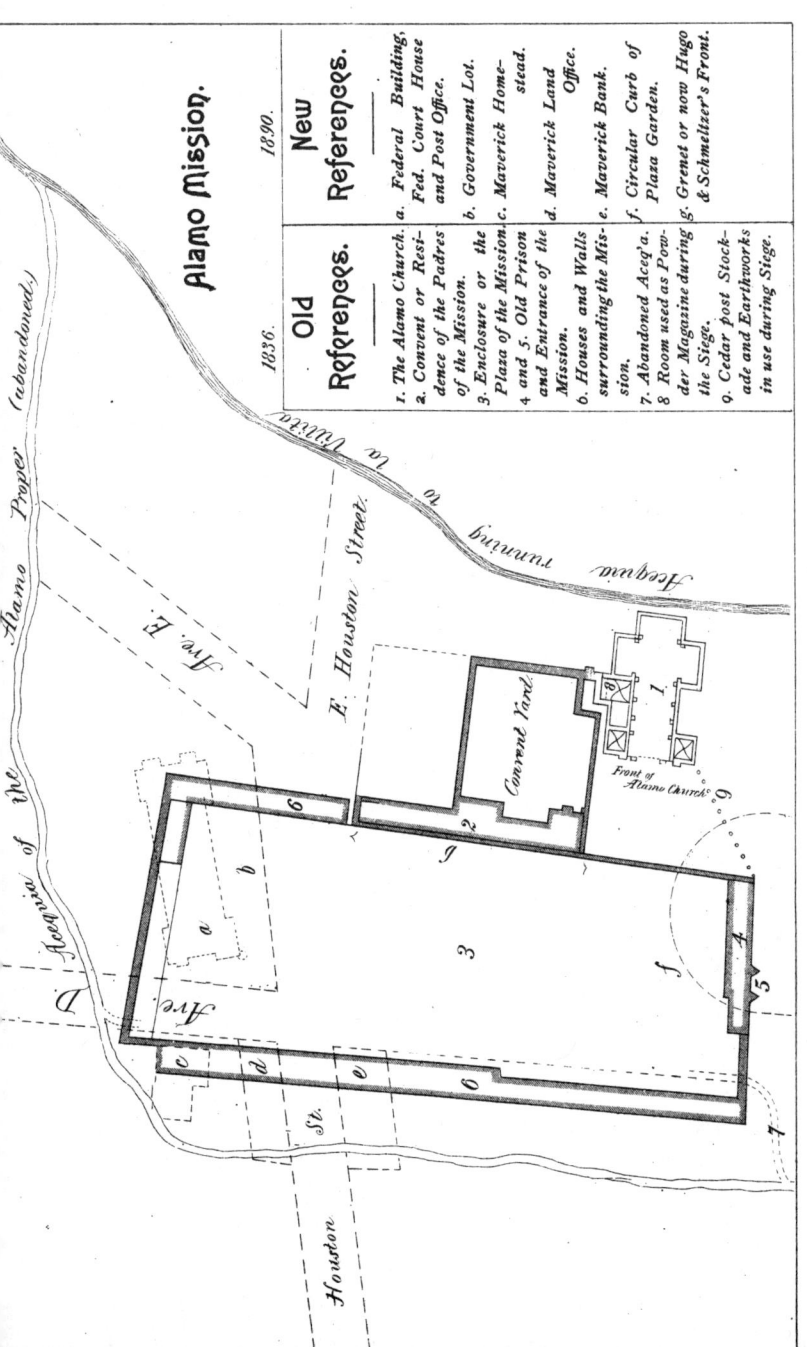

Plan of Mission San Antonio de Valero, published by William Corner in 1890.

Mission San Francisco Xavier

During the years 1722-1726, San Antonio Mission had a short-lived sub-mission, named San Francisco Xavier de Nájera, which never got beyond the founding stage. It owed its origin to an extraordinary Indian chief of the Sana tribe, who bore the Spanish name of Juan Rodíguez. His followers lived with others of the same tribe and the Yerbipiames in a settlement near the Trinity River, known as Ranchería Grande.

While the Marqués de Aguayo was still in Coahuila, getting ready for his expedition into Texas, Chief Rodríguez paid him a visit and asked him to establish a separate mission near San Antonio for his tribesmen who numbered about 600. He then returned to San Antonio and waited there with some of his followers for the arrival of Aguayo.

When the latter and his imposing army reached San Antonio on April 4, 1721, he suggested to Rodríguez that he and his people join the Indians at Mission San Antonio; but the chief replied that this was not possible, because they were too numerous, and besides they were not on friendly terms with the mission Indians. The Marqués de Aguayo promised to found a mission for them later.

Chief Rodríguez then served as guide for Aguayo's march to eastern Texas; and after Aguayo had returned to San Antonio in January, 1722, the chief went to the Ranchería Grande and brought back fifty families of the Sanas for the new mission. On March 12, Aguayo founded a mission for them on a beautiful plain, midway between Missions San Antonio and San José on the east side of the San Antonio River, the same site that was later occupied by Mission Concepción.

Fr. Joseph González, the assistant of Fr. Hidalgo at Mission San Antonio, was present on this occasion, and promised to take care of the Indians from San Antonio until another father could be sent from the College of Querétaro. Fr. Espinosa, then guardian of the College, had promised to do that.

Aguayo sent a report of what he had done to the new Viceroy Casafuerte, who had just arrived in Mexico City with instructions to curtail expenses; and the viceroy informed Fr. Espinosa, that he could not disburse the customary aid for the founding of another new mission, nor the annual allowance of 450 pesos for another missionary. Neither could the College bear these expenses, replied Fr. Espinosa; the Sanas would be welcome at one of the other two missions.

In the meantime, at Mission San Antonio, Fr. González had begun a separate record book for the new mission; and he visited the Sanas regularly at their camp on the mission site. No doubt, the Indians erected a temporary chapel; and here Fr. González offered up holy Mass for them and instructed them.

Aguayo's Offer of Supplies

As governor, Aguayo had supplied the new mission community with necessities at his own expense; and he asked his successor to do the same till the mission was established on a firm footing. In 1725 the Marqués generously offered to supply everything needful, if one of the two missionaries stationed at Mission San Antonio would assume the care of the new mission. Both the viceroy and the guardian of the College accepted his offer; and Fr. Miguel Sevillano de Paredes, newly appointed Fr. President of the Querétaro missions in Texas, was sent to San Antonio with instructions to proceed with the establishment of the mission.

A few days after he arrived in January, 1726, Fr. Sevillano called Chief Rodríguez and his Indians to San Antonio to inform them that a mission would be built for them and they could have as their missionary either himself or his assistant Fr. Joseph Hurtado, Fr. González left San Antonio later that year.

Fr. Sevillano was surprised when only twelve Indians came. Many of the Sanas had gone back to the Ranchería Grande. The Fr. President was still more amazed, when Chief Rodríguez told him that he and his few remaining followers now preferred to stay at Mission San Antonio. They would be safer there against attacks of the Apaches, their enemies.

Attempts to Establish the Mission

Although a messenger was hastily sent to Saltillo to prevent the supplies from being sent, at least for the present, Fr. Sevillano made every possible effort to make Mission San Francisco Xavier a sub-mission of San Antonio. He invited the seven chiefs of the Sanas who were at Ranchería Grande to San Antonio, where they were feasted for three days; but they absolutely refused to settle down in a mission. Brother Juan de los Angeles was at the mission at this time. He knew the language of the Sanas, which was the same as that of the Tejas; but even he could not persuade them to change their mind.

If the Sanas would not come, perhaps the Yerbipiames would; and so Chief Rodríguez went with Governor Pérez de Almazán to the Ranchería Grande to see the Yerbipiames, among whom there were many apostates from the missions in eastern Texas, to persuade some of them to come to San Francisco Xavier. This attempt likewise failed.

Fr. Sevillano made one last effort, or intended to do so, by going in person to the Paquaches on the upper Nueces. The Apaches had recently made two severe attacks upon them. Nothing came of that plan either; and Fr. Sevillano was elected guardian of the College of Querétaro in 1727.

After 1726, a separate register for San Francisco was no longer kept at San Antonio. The sub-mission was merged with Mission San Antonio and absorbed by it; and Aguayo's generous offer could not be accepted. Some five years later, the three Querétaran missions in eastern Texas were moved to the San Antonio River; and one of them, Concepción, was established at or near the site which had been chosen for San Francisco Xavier.[18]

---

18. Castañeda, *op. cit.*, II, 160-163.

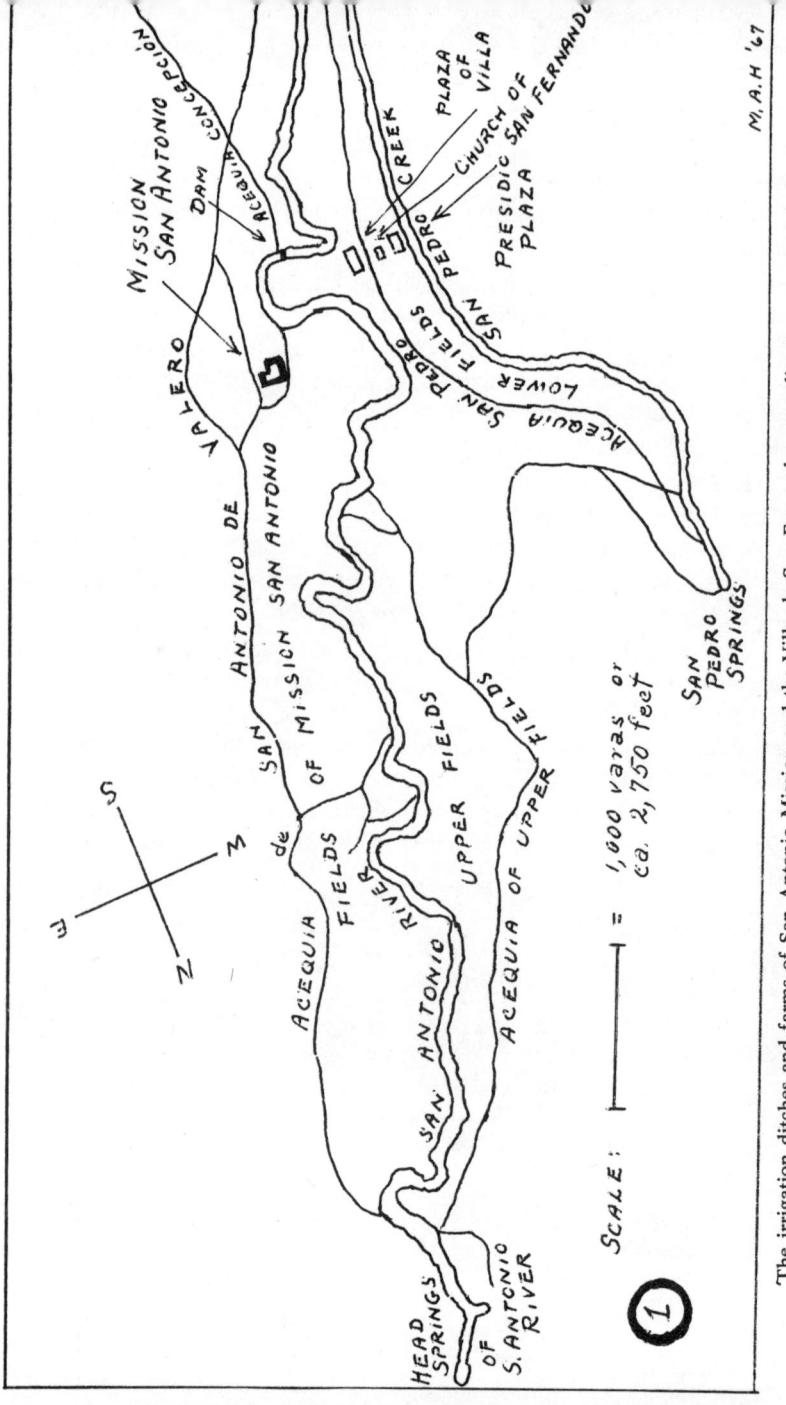

The irrigation ditches and farms of San Antonio Mission and the Villa de San Fernando, according to a map made by the Texas Civil Works Administration and the Texas Relief Commission. This map is continued on the three following pages.

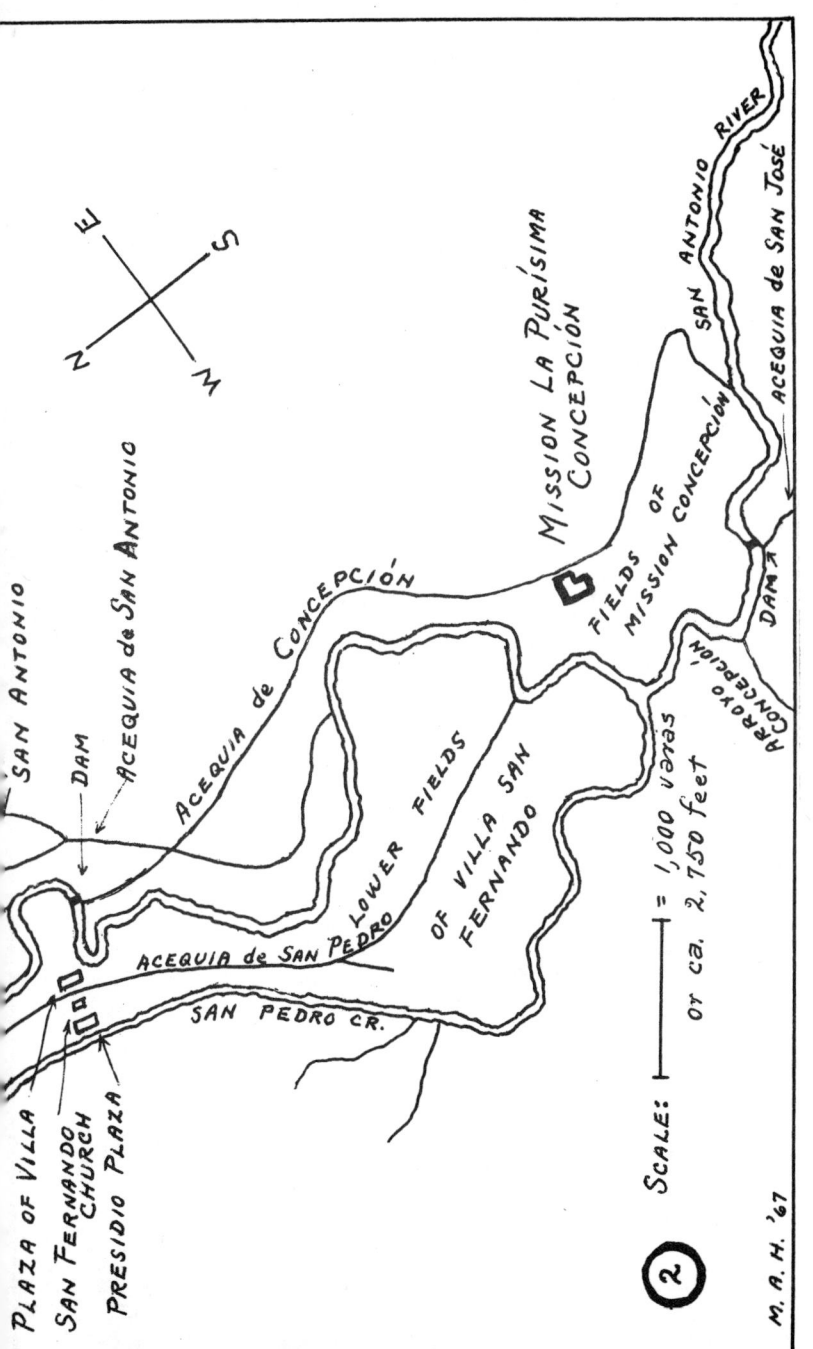

The irrigation ditches and farm of Purísima Concepción Mission.

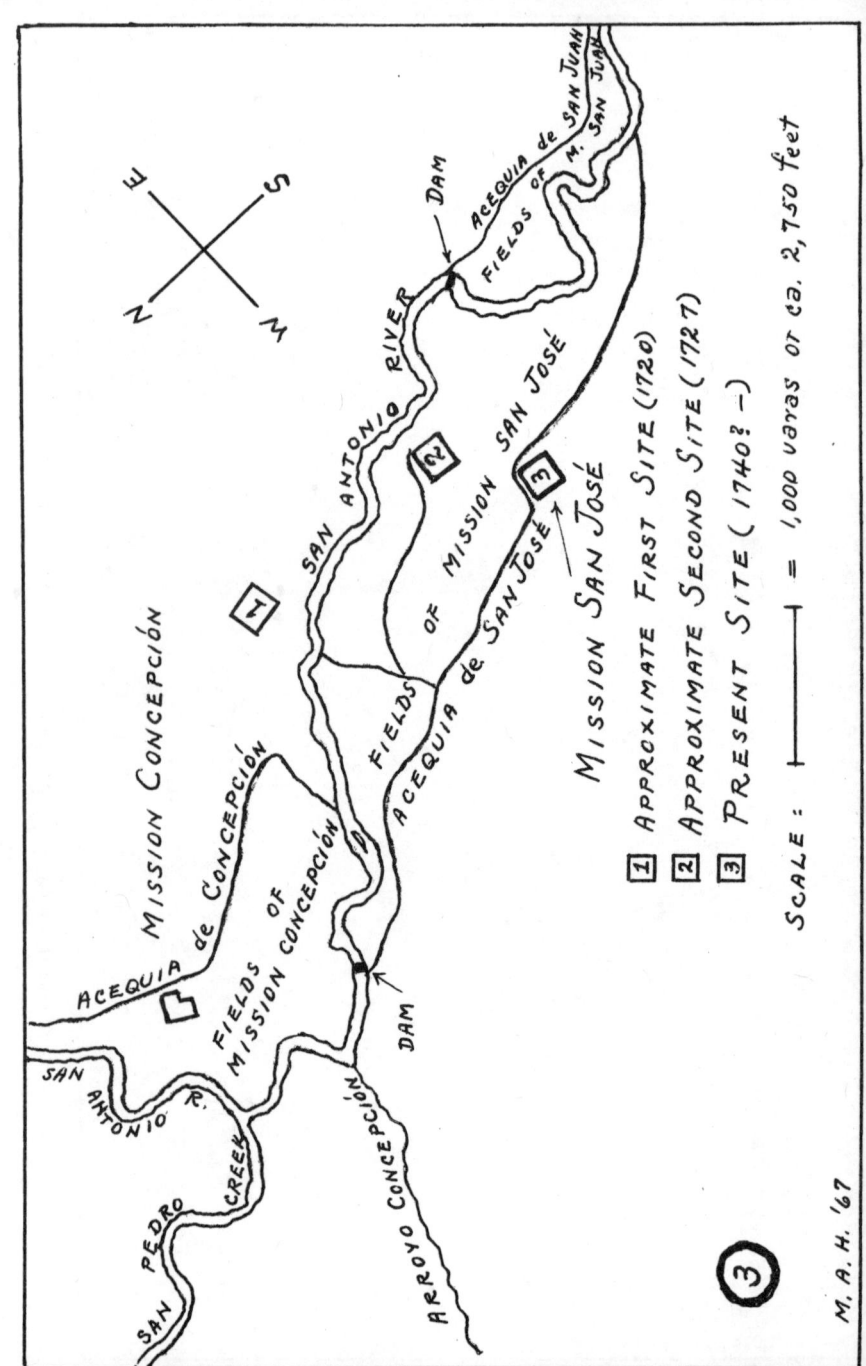

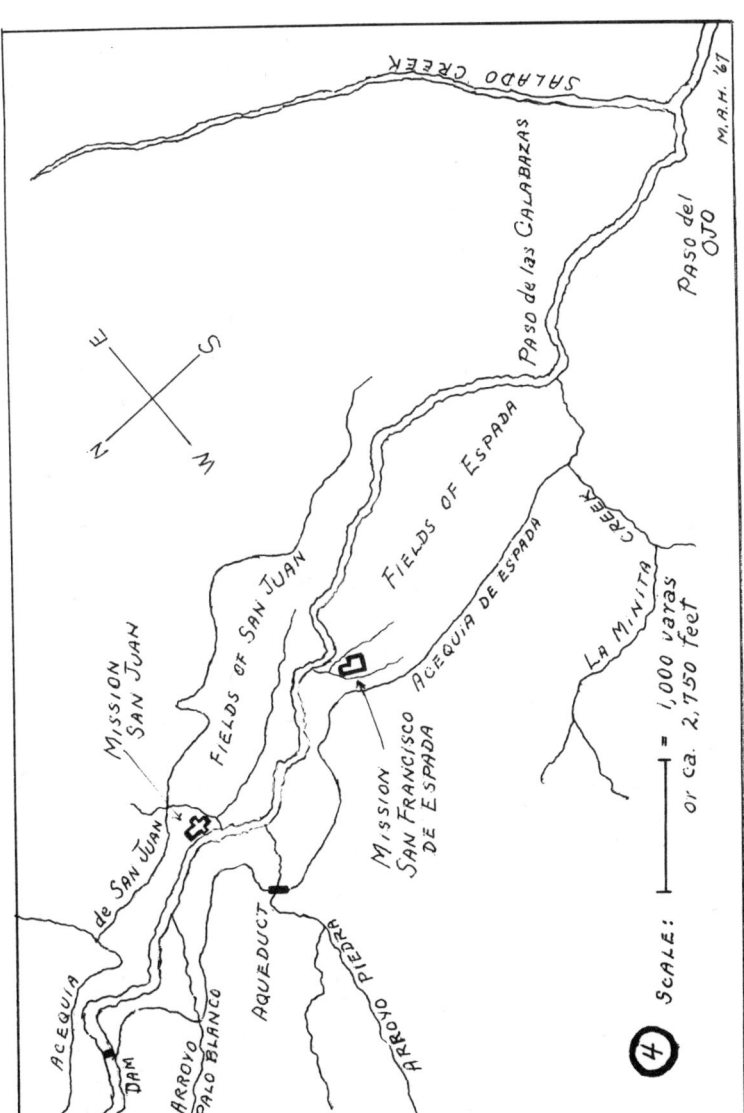

The irrigation ditches and farms of San Juan Capistrano and San Francisco de la Espada Missions.

Successors of Fr. Hidalgo

Fr. Joseph González, who had been Father Hidalgo's assistant, remained at Mission San Antonio until 1726. Because of his eagerness to begin missionary work among the Apaches, he became involved in a disagreement with Captain Flores of the presidio. According to Fr. Miguel Sevillano de Paredes, who visited San Antonio Mission in 1726 and 1727 and then was elected guardian of the College of Querétaro, Fr. Gonzalez "died while making a journey toward the missions of the Rio Grande" before August, 1728.[19]

When Brigadier General Rivera visited San Antonio in 1727, he found conditions at the presidio to be in good order; and at the mission, where Fr. Benito Sánchez was in charge, there were 273 resident Indians. While the building of a friary of stone had been commenced, the church was still a temporary structure. Much work had been done on an irrigation ditch two and a half miles long.

During the years 1728 to 1733, the missionary who made most of the entries in the baptismal register at Mission San Antonio was Fr. Juan Salvador de Amaya. As a Franciscan priest of the Province of Jalisco, he joined the College of Querétaro in 1728, and in the same year was assigned to the Mission of San Antonio. He served as a missionary in Texas for 24 years, until his death which occurred on November 17, 1752.

Fr. Benito de Santa Ana Fernández, who was the Fr. President of the Querétaran missions in Texas from 1733 to 1750, also resided at Mission San Antonio for three years before he became president and established his headquarters at Mission Nuestra Señora de la Purísima Concepción.

---

19. See the long letter written by Fr. Hidalgo on November 3, 1723, concerning Fr. González' efforts in behalf of the Apaches and his relations to Captain Flores, in R. F. Carter, *The Tarnished Halo: The Story of Padre Francisco Hidalgo* (Chicago, 1973), pp. 152-158. Cf. also "Missionaries at the San Antonio Mission" at the end of this booklet.

Both Fr. Amaya and Fr. Fernández had encounters with the Apaches who frequently attacked travelers and made raids on the missions and the presidio and settlement. On January 9, 1731, Fr. Amaya and Brother Francisco Bustamente were going with a small party from San Antonio to the Rio Grande when they were suddenly attacked by about fifty Apaches near the Medina River. The savages killed a woman and carried off a child. The others escaped with their lives, but lost their baggage and many of their horses and pack animals.

On June 25 of the same year, Fr. Fernández and Brother Estevan Sáenz Monge, were making the same trip with an escort of five soldiers when a band of Apaches swooped down upon them, killed two of the soldiers, and ran off with the baggage and all the horses. If Brother Estevan had not been wearing a leather shield he too would have been killed or wounded.

Another missionary of the San Antonio mission, Fr. Francisco de Frias, going to the Rio Grande, on September 20, 1736, with an escort of ten soldiers, met a large group of Apaches at Atascoso, about 35 miles south of San Antonio. They were able to hold off the enemy, although the captain of the soldiers and a friendly Indian were wounded. Fearful of another assault, they retraced their steps to San Antonio. Despite the persistent hostility of the Apaches, the missionaries were opposed to military campaigns against them. They hoped to establish friendly relations with them and to make Christians of them.

While Frs. Amaya and Fernández were at Mission San Antonio, in 1731, the Villa de Béxar at the presidio became the town of San Fernando. This development took place on March 9, when fifteen or sixteen families from the Canary Islands joined those who had already settled near the presidio.

In the same month and year, the three Querétaran missions of eastern Texas were moved to the San Antonio River, one between the San Antonio and San José missions, and the other two below the latter. Thus, within a distance of nine miles, there were now five missions.

Governor Franquis de Lugo

When General Rivera's recommendations were approved in 1729, the soldiers who were serving as guards at the missions in Texas were removed; but, at the request of the missionaries, these were restored the following year. In 1731 there were two soldiers at San Antonio, two at San José, and three at each of the other three on the San Antonio River.

The tempestuous Governor Carlos Franquis Benites de Lugo, who arrived in San Antonio in September, 1736, once more removed the guards at missions San Antonio and San José, and reduced the soldiers at the other three to one in each. After his short but stormy rule came to an end, Governor Orobio y Basterra sent the guards back to the missions.

In 1733 Fr. Mariano de los Dolores y Viana began his great missionary career of thirty years in Texas, principally at Mission San Antonio. Also after he was appointed the Fr. President of the Querétaran missions in 1750, he continued to reside at Mission San Antonio. In May, 1736, he built a bridge across the San Antonio River, using for this purpose six large beams which he had procured for repairs in the mission chapel. But the bridge was abused by the soldiers and settlers, who frequently came to the mission only to cause trouble.

On October 16, with the permission and orders of the Fr. President Fernández, Fr. Mariano had the bridge dismantled. That aroused the ire of Governor Franquis, who had the bridge rebuilt by forced Indian labor and threatened to pack Fr. Mariano on a mule and send him back to the College.[20] Fr. Mariano retired to Mission Concepción and then to Mission San Juan Capistrano, but after Governor Franquis was removed from office he went back to Mission San Antonio. In the mission's baptismal register there are numerous entries for the years 1739-1757 that were signed by Fr. Mariano.

The Epidemic of 1739

A virulent epidemic swept through the San Antonio area in 1739. Many of the mission Indians died and many others fled to the woods. The number of Indians at Mission San Antonio, which had been 300 before the plague, was reduced in 1739 to 184. But the missions recovered quickly. By the end of 1740, Mission San Antonio once more had 238 Indians.

Some of these Indians belonged to the Tacame tribe. Originally they had belonged to San José Mission, but they abandoned it in a group. Later, in 1736, they joined the Indians at the Espada Mission; but the following year they wanted to move to San Antonio. Not obtaining permission, they deserted

---

20. Castañeda, *op. cit.*, III, 49-66.

once more. The missionaries tried in vain to bring them back. However, in the winter of 1739 and the spring of 1740, the missionaries of San José, by making repeated trips, were able to conduct 77 Tacames to Mission San Antonio.

In the spring of 1740 Fr. President Fernández reported that the missions in the San Antonio area were all faring well, but San Antonio de Valero, the oldest of them, had the largest and best organized pueblo of Indians.[21]

At the end of the same year, in a letter to the viceroy, Captain Toribio de Urrutia praised the work of the missionaries, but noted that the mission buildings, including those of Mission San Antonio, were still only of a temporary nature. The churches had only thatched roofs of straw. A note in the baptismal register of Mission San Antonio records the fact that the first stone of the mission's first stone church was laid on May 8, 1744.

---

21. Fr. Benito Fernández de Santa Ana, "Descripcion de las misiones . . . , Feb. 20, 1740," in Biblioteca Nacional, Mexico City, translated by B. Leutenegger, in "Two Franciscan Documents on Early San Antonio, Texas," *The Americas*, XXV, No. 2 (October, 1968), 199-206. The other document is the letter Fr. Olivares wrote in 1716 to the viceroy concerning the Indians of Texas.

Painting of the Alamo as it looked about 1847, by Theodore Gentilz (in Texas 1844-1906), first of a series depicting all five of the San Antonio missions. The other four are reproduced on the pages which follow.

Painting of Purísima Concepción Mission by Theodore Gentilz.

Painting of San José Mission by Theodore Gentilz

Painting of San Juan Capistrano Mission by Theodore R. Davis

Painting of San Francisco de la Espada Mission by Theodore Gentilz.

Visit of Fr. Ortiz, 1745

The very next year Fr. Francisco Xavier Ortiz came from Querétaro to inspect the missions of this college in Texas. For more than a month he lived in San Antonio, made a thorough investigation of the status of the four Querétaran missions, and prepared a detailed report.[22]

He mentions the fact that a new church of stone and mortar was being built at a distance of two gun shots east of the church of San Fernando. The earlier church, probably an adobe structure, had fallen down; and while the new church was under construction, a large (adobe) hall was being used as a church. In this temporary church, there were two confessionals, two benches, and an altar with a carved statue of St. Anthony about one *vara* (ca. 2 feet, 9 inches) high and above it a crucifix that was twice as large.

In an adjoining room, used as a sacristy, there was another altar with a statue of the Immaculate Conception of the same size as that of St. Anthony. In the sacristy were kept twelve large pictures or paintings which were to be placed in the new church and four large bells for its tower.

The friary or residence of the missionaries was a two-story structure of stone and mortar. On the ground floor were offices and other rooms (kitchen and dining room), and on the second floor three private rooms.

Adjoining the friary, was the textile shop, with three looms, six pairs of cards, eight combs, six shuttles, and twenty spinning wheels. It had an open gallery. Here the Indian women and others who could not work on the farm manufactured excellent sackcloth, coarse cotton weaves, and brown domestic fabrics. The wool was provided by the mission's flock of sheep and the cotton came from its fields.

---

22. Fr. Francisco Xavier Ortiz, "Visita de las misiones . . . 1745," in Archives of the College of Querétaro, Mexico. Transcript in University of Texas Library; copy in RLSJ.

There was also a carpenter shop, a blacksmith shop, and chisels and hammers for the stone masons. Next to the textile shop stood the granary, where the corn harvest and other grain was stored, and beyond it several office rooms.

The mission Indians, who numbered 311 (275 baptized and 36 under instruction), lived in two long rows of huts, built of adobe bricks and roofed with straw. They stood on both sides of the irrigation ditch which ran through the mission compound; and along each row there was a sort of street.

The mission had 23 yokes of oxen for cultivating the fields of the mission farm. It was irrigated by a large *acequia* or ditch which led the water from the river to the fields. The annual corn crop in good years, grown from 8 to 9 *fanegas* (about 12-4/5 to 14-1/3 bushels) of seed, was 1,000 to 1,200 *fanegas* (1,600 to 1,920 bushels). Two *fanegas* (about 3-1/2 bushels) of beans yielded 60 *fanegas* (about 96 bushels). Two fields of cotton produced about 40 *arrobas* (1,000 pounds). Two or three patches were used to grow watermelons, melons, and pumpkins.

The pasture land which lay east and north of the mission was a big ranch with about 2,300 head of cattle, 1,317 sheep, and 304 goats. While Fr. Ortiz was at the mission, an actual count of the cattle was made; 2,002 head were counted, but the rest could not be counted because of the nearness of Apaches. The Indian cowboys of the mission did their work with the aid of forty horses. San Antonio Mission had its own branding iron, and the branding took place once a year.

Since its founding, Mission San Antonio had made a large number of Indian converts. Its registers showed that the missionaries had baptized a total of 981 Indians and had given Christian burial to 685.

Not satisfied with seeing the remarkable achievements of the mission with his own eyes, and to provide an answer to the false accusations which were lodged at times against the missionaries, Fr. Ortiz submitted a questionnaire on the conduct of the missionaries to a representative group of officials and settlers in San Antonio on June 25, 1745.

All testified that the missionaries had been and were toiling selflessly and indefatigably for the temporal and spiritual welfare of the natives but the missions were by no means ready for secularization. With much kindness and patience, the missionaries gradually induced the Indians to overcome their natural laziness and to work for a living.

Besides devoting themselves faithfully to the sacred ministry, the missionaries often performed the most menial tasks in order to encourage the Indians by their example. The inborn repugnance of the Indians to systematic labor was the reason why some of them, even after they had become Christians, sometimes ran off to the freedom of the wilds. To bring new Indian converts into the missions, the missionaries made journeys to points that were more than 200 leagues (about 520 miles) distant. The distance probably included the return trip.

The Apache Indians

Fr. Ortiz was probably still in San Antonio five days later (June 30, 1745), when a force of 350 Ypandi and Natage Apaches (including women and children) made an attack on the presidio and the town of San Fernando. It happened during the night. While some of the Indians remained in ambush outside the town, others went up to the presidio to set fire to it.

Fortunately a boy discovered them and gave the alarm. The citizens and soldiers were able to hold the enemy at bay for a time; but then the Indians divided into separate groups and made attacks at different places at the same time. The Spaniards would surely have succumbed, if at the critical moment one hundred Indians from Mission San Antonio de Valero had not come to their rescue. The Apaches were not only repelled but routed; and the Spaniards and mission Indians pursued them as far as a place called Buenavista, where the victors were ordered back.

Concerning this attack on San Antonio, Dr. Castañeda wrote: "The fate of Fort St. Louis (the French settlement of Lavaca Bay which was destroyed by the Karankawas in 1689) might have been the fate of San Antonio de Béjar, had it not been for the timely aid of the mission Indians of Valero and the friendly policy of Fr. Benito Fernández de Santa Ana. The cackling of geese saved Rome; the loyalty of the recently converted Indians of today's Alamo saved San Antonio in 1745. No more eloquent proof of the success of the missionaries in Christianizing and civilizing the wild children of the plains can be found."[23]

On November 28, 1749, a peace treaty between the Spaniards and Apaches was ratified in San Antonio amid elaborate ceremonies; but it was a treaty which many of the Apaches did not keep. They continued to be a menace and a danger to the end of the Spanish period, and even into the Mexican and American periods. But the missionaries of the College of Querétaro were not daunted. They did everything they possibly could to make them Christians, friends, and civilized, law-abiding citizens.

They began by establishing a short-lived mission for the Apaches of Texas in Coahuila, 1754-1755. In the latter year almost a thousand Apaches joined the two Querétaran missions on the San Marcos River. These missions, plus a third

---

23. Castañeda, *op. cit.*, III, 48-49.

mission, had been founded originally in 1748-1749 on the San Gabriel River for various tribes of the Tejas Indians. Two of these missions were moved in 1755 to the San Marcos; and the following year one of them, San Francisco Xavier, the only one that remained, was continued on the Guadalupe near New Braunfels. But it too come to an end in 1758.

In the meantime, in 1757, the Apache mission of San Sabá was established near Menard with the cooperation of the College of San Fernando in Mexico City. It was destroyed the very next year by the Comanches and other northern tribes; and two missionaries died as martyrs.

Another attempt was made in 1762, when two Apache missions were founded on the Nueces. Two years later each of them had over 400 neophytes; but after seven years, these also had to be given up.

In these endeavors Fr. Mariano de los Dolores of Mission San Antonio, who was named the Fr. President of the Querétaran missions of Texas in 1750, played an important role. If the missionaries did not succeed in making Christians of the Apaches, it was not due to any failure on their part to do their level best and that with an amazing preseverance.

Ambulatory alongside the restored section of the convento or missionaries' residence and the workshops of San Antonio Mission.

Second Visit of Fr. Ortiz, 1756

In 1756 the same Fr. Ortiz who had visited the missions in 1745 returned to make another inspection.[24] At Mission San Antonio he found that the stone church which was begun in 1744 had been completed, but it had been poorly constructed and had fallen down completely. It was now being rebuilt, and in the meantime an adobe hall was being used as a church.

The friary was a two-story structure, with four rooms on the second floor and on the ground floor a guest room and various offices. On the second floor there was a door leading to the choir loft of the church.

At the place where the mission had stood in 1719-1724, the mission still had a stone chapel, 11 by 4 *varas* (about 30 by 11 feet), in which there was a stone cross that was greatly venerated. This chapel, called Capilla de la Santa Cruz, was fitted out for divine services, and holy Mass was celebrated in it sometimes.

In the mission square there were 30 Indian houses of adobe, of which 20 had open galleries with stone arches. Additional Indian quarters were still *jacales,* huts of brush; but new ones like the others were being built. No less than 328 Indians were living in the mission, the largest number in its history. An *acequia* ran through the square. The textile shop had four looms.

For work on the farm there were 24 yokes of oxen. On the ranch were 1,000 head of cattle, 2,050 sheep, 50 swine, 100 horses, and 50 mares. The horses were used by the cowboys and shepherds.

---

24. Fr. Francisco Xavier Ortiz, *Razón de la Visita de las Misiones . . . Maio de 1756.* This is a facsimile reprint, made in 1955, of the original printing of this report, of which a copy is in the Archivo del Museo, Mexico. One of the 75 copies made in 1955, in three small volumes (42, 33, and 45 pp.), is in the DRT Library at the Alamo; and a copy is in RLSJ. Castañeda was unaware of the existence of this important report on San Antonio de Valero and the other missions in the area as well as the San Xavier Missions. So far, a manuscript copy of Fr. Ortiz' Report of 1756 has not been found.

Since 1703, when the mission was first established on the other side of the Rio Grande, the records showed that 1,279 had been baptized, 944 had received Christian burial, and 308 had entered Christian marriages.

Although the second stone church of Mission San Antonio, which was under construction in 1756, was never completed while the mission was in existence, this was done in the nineteenth century. The date on the façade, 1757, can still be seen. Already in 1758 Governor Jacinto Barrios reported that considerable progress had been made. It was to be a large church of cut stone, with a transept and two towers.

Concerning this, the second stone church of Mission San Antonio, Fr. Mariano de los Dolores wrote in 1762: "Although the church of this mission (the one which was begun in 1744) had been completely finished, including a tower and sacristy, it fell to the ground because of the poor skill of the architect; and another of harmonious design is now being built with quarried stone which is found almost on the spot. It has the solidity and perfection that is required for beauty and for the support of the vaults."

Early in 1759,[25] the governors of the provinces of Coahuila and Texas met with Colonel Ortiz Parilla to plan a campaign against the hostile northern tribes. Authorized no doubt to do so by the College, Fr. Mariano took the occasion to present to the governors a formal offer to surrender to them the temporal administration of the four Querétaran missions on the Rio de San Antonio and the two on the Rio Grande.

---

25. From the *Libros de los Muertos* in the Archives of the College of Querétaro it is evident that Fr. Mariano de los Dolores y Viana died in 1763, not after 1769, as the writer stated in the first edition of *The Alamo Chain of Missions*. This error was due to another in Castañeda, IV, 259, where the date of the meeting of the governors of Coahuila and Texas in San Antonio with Colonel Ortiz Parilla is given as "early in 1769." The meeting, at which Fr. Dolores y Viana offered the missionaries' resignation of the temporal administration of the missions (an offer that was not accepted) took place in 1759, not 1769.

It was a challenging proposal and a demolishing reply to the false charges repeatedly made against the missionaries that they were more interested in accumulating wealth than in saving the souls of Indians. If they accepted the offer, Fr. Mariano warned them, it would henceforth be their responsibility to protect and increase the possessions of the missions, which belonged to the Indians. In their reply, the governors praised the efficient administration of the missionaries and said they could not consider the offer without first consulting the viceroy.

Report of 1762

On March 6, 1762, Fr. President Mariano de los Dolores sent to Fr. Francisco Xavier Ortiz, the same who had visited Texas in 1745 and 1756 and was now the Fr. Guardian of the College of Querétaro, a detailed report of all the missions under his jurisdiction. It is not just one report but a collection of reports, each one written by one of the missionaries who was in charge of one of the Querétaran missions in Texas.[26]

---

26. The 1762 report of Fr. Mariano de los Dolores and his fellow missionaries of the College of Querétaro is in the Archivo de la Nación, Mexico, Historia, vol. 28, folios 162-183. A copy that was formerly in the Library of the University of Texas, we have been told, is no longer there. Castañeda, *op. cit.*, IV, 4-11, has a sufficiently complete summary of the report.

A graphic picture of Mission San Antonio is presented in Fr. Mariano's description of his own mission as it was in 1762; and it indicates the improvements that had been made, despite the fact that the newly built church collapsed shortly after it was completed.

A new granary had been built. It was "a large stone building" in which "the supplies were kept. Here there was a room to store as many as 1,800 bushels of corn and several hundred bushels of beans, which were the annual harvest raised by the mission Indians." This is Castañeda's translation (*op. cit.,* IV, 5-6); and since a *fanega* is the equivalent of 1.6 bushel (not 2 bushels, as he thought), 1,800 bushels should be reduced to 1,440.

The second stone church of the mission, begun in 1756 after the first had collapsed, was still under construction in 1762. After the new granary was completed, the old granary, which was 35 *varas* (about 96 feet) long, was converted into a temporary church. It had two altars, one with a crucifix, 1-1/3 *varas* (about 3-1/3 feet) in length, and a carved statue of St. Anthony, one *vara* (about 1-1/3 feet) high, standing in a niche. The second altar had an artistically clothed statue of Our Lady of Sorrows, which was taken down once a week and carried in an outdoor procession during which the Indians recited the Rosary. In the choir of the church there was a third altar with a statue of Jesus of Nazareth and benches along the sides.

In the church were two benches, two confessionals, a holy water font, and a copper baptismal font with a cover. There were also four large church bells. A separate room, adjoining the church, served as a sacristy. Among its furnishings were fourteen complete sets of vestments and four copes.

The little stone chapel at the second site of the mission was still there and equipped with all that was needed for the celebration of holy Mass.

The new granary and the temporary church, together with the houses of the Indians and various workshops formed a large rectangular walled enclosure. On the south side there was a fortified gate, and above it a turret in which three cannons were installed. The Indian houses, built of stone against the walls, had arched porticoes and were arranged in seven rows or tiers; and on the west side of the plaza there was flowing water, connected with the irrigation canal and shaded by willows and fruit trees.

The Indian quarters were all provided with doors and windows, with beds raised above the ground, with chests having drawers, and with the necessary household utensils. The latter included a *metate* (a stone for grinding corn), a *comal* (a flat iron to make corn bread), and pots and pans. Inside the enclosure a good well had been dug to provide drinking water.

The friary and textile shop formed a separate little square on the east side of the large rectangular enclosure. This smaller square was about 50 *varas* (about 137-1/2 feet) long on two sides.

"Back of the friary," there was a large hall in which there were four looms, and adjoining it two store rooms where the wool, cotton, combs, cards, and spools were kept. In this workshop the Indian women manufactured cotton and woolen cloth and blankets of various kinds.

The friary was a two-story stone building, with private rooms, a dining room, a kitchen, and offices, all of which were flanked by open archways facing the patio. Outside the friary square, the new church was being built, with its main entrance facing west.

Irrigation canals, with stone trenches, ran along both the west and the east sides outside the two enclosures and supplied water for the fenced mission farm, on which corn, beans, chile, cotton, and some vegetables were raised. The mission had forty yokes of oxen, thirty plows, and other implements for cultivating the soil, and also twelve carts for transporting stone, timber, and other supplies.

On the mission ranch there were 115 saddle horses, 1,015 head of cattle, 2,300 sheep and goats, 200 mares, 15 donkeys, and 18 mules. Since the ranch was at some distance from the mission compound, a stone house and a stone chapel had been constructed on the site for the cowboys and shepherds and their families. The ranch house, which was 25 *varas* (about 69 feet) long, had three rooms and an arcade. Its chapel was 11 *varas* (about 30 feet) long; it had an altar with a stone cross two *varas* (about 5-1/2 feet) high, and two sets of vestments for the celebration of holy Mass.

The total number of mission Indians in 1762 was 275 or 76 families. All were Christians except 32 who were still receiving instructions and preparing for baptism. The various tribes represented among them were the Jarames, Payayas, Zanas, Apaches (Yprandes), Cocos, Tops, and Karankawas.

Since the founding of the mission near the Rio Grande the number of Indians baptized was 1,572. Those who had received Christian burial numbered 1,247; and the total of Christian marriages was 454. The Bureau of American Ethnology's *Handbook of American Indians* is mistaken when it says that Fr. Mariano indulged in an "obvious exaggeration" of the number of converted Indians. The register of baptisms of Mission San Antonio, which is in the Archives of San Fernando Cathedral in San Antonio shows that Fr. Mariano reported the number of entries that he found in the mission's registers. Included were the baptisms that had been administered during the years 1703 to 1718, because San Antonio Mission was a continuation of the earlier one on the Rio Grande.

Carefully recorded in the baptismal register of Mission San Antonio is the name of every Indian who was baptized, the day on which this was done, and the signature of the missionary who administered the sacrament. The first three baptisms at San Antonio Mission were those of dying children, the first by Fr. Miguel Núñez de Haro, the second by Fr. Olivares, and the third by Brother Pedro Maleta. The record of baptisms ends with the year 1783; and so, the entries for the last ten years of the mission's existence are missing.

Fr. Mariano Viana concluded his account of Mission San Antonio by mentioning that, besides himself, its missionaries in 1762 were Fr. José López and Brother Juan de los Angeles. Fr. José López of the College of Querétaro must be distinguished from Fr. José Francisco López of the College of Zacatecas, who was in charge of Mission San Antonio later on and, like his namesake, held the office of *presidente*.

Fr. José López seems to have succeeded Fr. Mariano Viana as Fr. President in 1763. We find him at Mission Concepción in 1764. He may also have substituted for the Fr. President in 1760, when Fr. Mariano Viana traveled all the way to Mexico City in a vain attempt to prevent the return of Felipe de Rábago y Terán to Texas as the captain of the Presidio de San Luís de las Amarillas.

The successor of Fr. José López was Fr. Asisclos Valverde, and he served as president from 1764 to 1770. He was followed by Fr. Juan Joseph Sáenz de Gumiel, the last of the Querétaran presidents in Texas.

One of the last missionaries of the College of Santa Cruz de Querétaro who was stationed at Mission San Antonio de Valero was Fr. Manuel Carrasco. It was Fr. Carrasco who in July, 1772, with only two Christian companions, had made a journey to the Lipan-Apaches in search of runaway Indians and had brought back eight apostates. Captain Rafael Martínez Pacheco declared that "he might have returned with all the runaways, if he had been given an adequate (military) escort, as had been done in the past."

An old photograph of the Alamo (San Antonio Mission church), taken about 1874.

Zacatecan Friars at San Antonio

The Querétaran friars left the Texas mission field in 1773; and their four missions on the San Antonio River passed into the care of the missionaries of the College of Zacatecas. Those of Querétaro departed regretfully, in order to devote themselves to missionary work in the former Jesuit missions of Pimería Alta (northern Mexico and southern Arizona); and there they developed a flourishing chain of missions similar to the contemporary missions of the College of San Fernando in Alta California. Their missions of San Juan Bautista and San Bernardo on the Rio Grande were entrusted at this time to the Franciscan Province of Guadalajara.

Only recently the *inventarios* of the four missions of San Antonio, Concepción, San Juan, and Espada, drawn up in December, 1772, were found at Guadalupe, Zacatecas. They prove that the Fr. President who surrendered these Querétaran missions to the College of Zacatecas was, not Fr. Diego Jiménez, but Fr. Juan Joseph Sáenz de Gumiel. Fr. Jiménez was president only of the missions in Coahuila which extended across the Rio Grande into Texas and had included the missions among the Apaches; but the president of the San Antonio chain of missions (except San José), in the province of Texas, was Fr. Sáenz de Gumiel in 1772. The latter had been a missionary in Texas for eight years, twice served as the Fr. Guardian of the College of Querétaro, and died there at the age of 83, on March 11, 1807.[27]

---

27. Castañeda, *op. cit.*, IV, 267, is mistaken when he says that in 1772 Fr. Diego Jiménez "was president of the missions on the Rio Grande and San Antonio." His jurisdiction had extended to the two Texas missions for the Apaches which were in existence 1762-1769 on the Nueces River, because this territory belonged to the Province of Coahuila. The missions on the San Antonio River, in the Province of Texas, had their own Fr. President, namely Fr. Sáenz de Gumiel. The four *inventarios* prepared by the latter, with an English translation by Fr. Benedict Leutenegger, are being printed at the present time (1977) as one of the reports of the State Archeologist and a publication of the Texas Historical Survey Committee, Austin. Copies of the *inventarios* are in RLSJ.

The Zacatecan missionaries, in 1773, already had the care of Mission San José and the two at La Bahía; and in that same year they were forced to abandon their three missions in eastern Texas. Thus they were able to take over Mission San Antonio and the other three missions without difficulty.

The first Zacatecan friar to be placed in charge of Mission San Antonio was Fr. Joseph Francisco Mariano de la Garza. He was followed in 1777 by Fr. José María Salas, who was transferred to San José Mission in 1783. The next missionary of San Antonio was Fr. José Francisco López, who became Fr. President of the Texas missions a few years later and remained at San Antonio until 1793.

The rapid decline of Mission San Antonio had already begun when it became a Zacatecan mission. Its decline was not due to the fact that another College was placed in charge, as some have thought. The true reasons were pointed out by Fr. López in his report of 1789. But before we give our attention to that report, we must mention Teodoro de Croix' visit to San Antonio in 1777-1778.

Fr. Morfi's Account of San Antonio

During his tour of inspection of the entire frontier of New Spain, De Croix was accompanied by Fr. Juan Agustín Morfi; and after he returned to Mexico, the latter wrote the first *History of Texas, 1673-1779*. In this work he gives an account of Mission San Antonio as he found it at the time of his visit.

It agrees for the most part with Fr. Mariano Viana's description written in 1762.

We learn, however, that the sacristy of the new church had been completed and was being used as a church while the church itself was still under construction. "The church," he writes, "was ruined through the ignorance of the builder; but a new one, simple, roomy, and well planned, is being erected on the same spot, though it is not finished. In the meantime services are held in the sacristy, which is a small room, but very tidy and neat, with a small new golden altar, where a handsome image of the patron St. Anthony is venerated."[28]

Fr. Morfi also throws some light on the location of the textile shop and indicates that when Fr. Mariano said the friary was 50 *varas* square he included not only the friary proper (which was only half as large) but also its "backyard," that is, a second patio of the same size, on the north side of the friary.

The mission, says Fr. Morfi, "has a small friary, 50 *varas* square, with an arched gallery around the patio, on the first and the second floors, around which have been built the necessary rooms for the missionaries with the usual porter's lodge, refectory, offices, and kitchen; and in the second patio, there is a large room with four looms and the necessary spinning wheels to weave cotton cloth for shawls and ordinary coarse cotton and woolen cloth for the Indians. Two other rooms, in which the raw materials and the tools are kept, adjoin the workshop." Actually, therefore, each of the two smaller squares or patios must have been about 25 *varas* square (about 69 feet square).

"At the entrance to the friary," Fr. Morfi adds, "a small

---

28. Fr. Juan Agustín Morfi's Historia de la Provincia de Texas, translated into English by C. E. Castañeda, with introduction and notes, was published as *History of Texas, 1673-1779, by Fray Juan Agustín Morfi*, 2 vols. or parts (page numbers continued in Part II), Albuquerque, 1935.

watchtower was built, with three loopholes for three swivel guns, which, with other firearms and their ammunition, are carefully guarded."

Fr. Morfi also supplies the information that since 1762 the number of mission Indians "has been greatly reduced, and today (1778) the mission has scarcely enough of them to cultivate the fields; and the looms have been abandoned" because of the lack of workers. According to a census made in 1777, only 44 Indians were living at Mission San Antonio, far less than in any of the other missions. Little wonder, then, that the new church could not be completed.

The mission farm was being cultivated, at least to some extent with the aid of Spanish labor; and the missionary was able to give these farmhands only relatively low wages. However, the missionary of San Antonio continued his efforts to bring in new Indian converts to the very end, and he did succeed in assembling a few of them.

In the course of the following decade, too, a fairly large settlement of families grew up just southeast of the mission compound. They were called *agregados* or squatters; and many of the mission Indians intermarried with these settlers. This settlement was called La Villita, at least later on; and eventually it formed an important part of the town of San Fernando and the city of San Antonio.

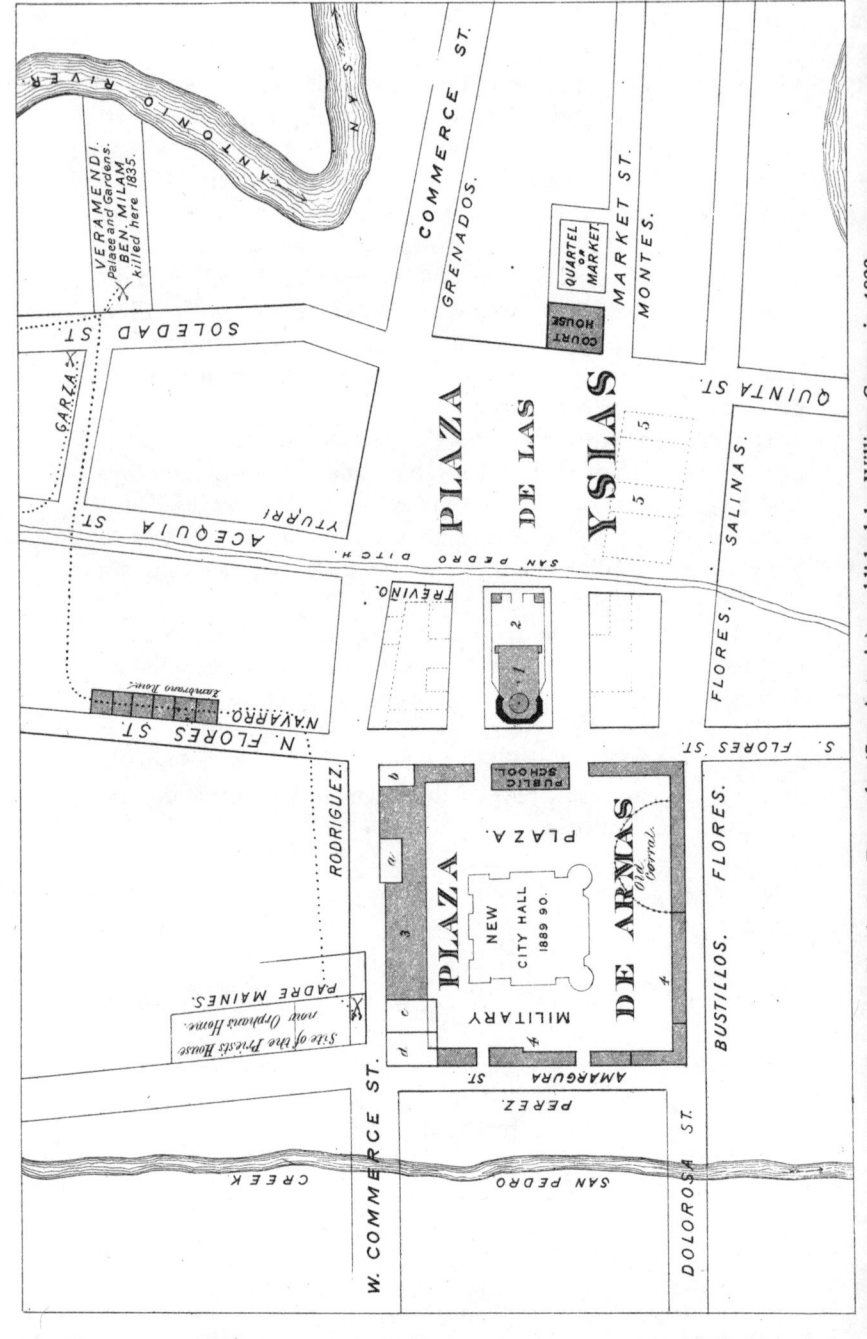

References

Illustrating the Villa Capital de San Fernando, Spanish Garrison, Etc.

---

1. The old Church of San Fernando.
2. Churchyard Burying Ground, now covered by the Cathedral of 1868-72.
3. The Presidio Garrison Barracks, long since removed.
4. The old Plaza de Armas Dwellings and Ramparts. All 3 and 4 were claimed by the city as city property and in most cases the city substantiated its claims, and, acquiring it, cleared the old buildings away. The lot marked *b* was the last private property to disappear–1889. In the '40s and '50s a man named Goodman gave much trouble before he was finally ousted by law by the city. Plats of most of these properties, and the names of claimants, may be found in Book 1, City Engineer's Records. The City Hall of 1850-90, with City Jail, occupied N. W. corner, *c d*.
5. Properties of N. Lewis, Callaghan, Groesbeeck, et al., on Main Plaza, claimed and cleared by the city similarly to those on Military Plaza (See note 4).
6. The isolated Spanish family names on the plan are those of some of the original property holders.
7. The faintly dotted lines to and from the Veramendi and Garza Houses are the approximate routes to Zambrano Row and to the Priest House taken by the besieging companies under Milam and F. W. Johnston in 1835. The capitulation of Cos to Burleson followed in 1835.

This plan is about 75 varas to the inch, Rampart Dwellings from 6 to 12 varas wide, Garrison Barracks, 20 varas wide.

Report of Fr. López, 1789

In 1789 Mission San Antonio had more resident Indians than in 1777. This we learn from the carefully prepared and illuminating report which Fr. José Francisco López wrote at Mission San Antonio and signed on March 5, 1789.[29] After presenting a detailed account of the seven missions of Texas which were then still in the care of the missionaries of the Zacatecas College, he frankly and clearly points out the true reasons for their sharp decline.

The principal reason, he declares, was the decree which Teodoro de Croix issued after his visit in 1777-1778. This decree appropriated all unbranded cattle, making them government property; and it required everyone, the missions included, who took or slaughtered any such cattle to pay a fee of four *reales* (one half a peso) per head. The wealth of the missions had consisted principally in their cattle. The Apaches had stolen all but a few of their horses, and hence they had been unable to round up the cattle and brand them.

As a result, the missions were impoverished overnight. To feed the Indians they had to buy their own cattle from the government with the corn they raised. Thus several vicious circles ensued; and the missions were unable to assemble and take care of a large number of Indians within their walls. There were other contributing causes, enumerated by Fr. López, but the principal one was the loss of the mission cattle. His report is one last urgent plea that the situation be remedied and the missions saved from extinction, but it failed to achieve its purpose.

The account of Mission San Antonio shows that this mission was still in a fairly good condition. All it needed was more mission Indians, but it was now impotent to gather them. The mission, writes Father López, "is built to form almost a

---

29. Fr. José Francisco López, Razón e Ynforme . . . May 5, 1789, translated into English by J. Autry Dabbs, published as *The Texas Missions in 1785* (sic), *Texas Catholic Historical Society Preliminary Studies*, III, no. 6 (Austin, 1940).

square [an irregular rectangle], surrounded by a single stone and mud wall that stands about 300 paces from the center. The same rampart serves as a wall for most of the fifteen or sixteen houses, with ample capacity for lodging the Indians. Nearly all the houses are covered with wood and mortar, as a protection against the rain; and they have handcarved, wooden doors with locks and iron keys. Within the square is the granary, made of stone and lime, which has enough room to hold 2,000 *fanegas* (about 3,200 bushels) of corn, several hundred *fanegas* of beans, etc.

"Next [outside the square, adjoining it on the east side] is the house or living quarters, adequate for the missionary and the officers of the community, made of stone and lime, with good roofs, doors, windows, and locks.

"Adjoining this building, is the sacristy which serves today as the church [that is, the sacristy of the new church, on its north side], while another room [next to the sacristy, on its west side] now serves as the sacristy. Both structures are of stone and mortar, and are built with arched roofs.

"This mission has under construction a church with a very large nave [and a transept]; the walls of the nave are built as high as the cornices, but the latter have been built only in the dome of the sanctuary. In the front, its beautiful façade of sculptured stone has been completed to the same height as the walls. . . . [Because of the lack of mission Indians and for other reasons] it cannot now be carried on to completion.

"The lowest evaluation that may be placed upon the church and sacristy is 20,000 pesos, with an additional 8,000 for the furnishings and ornaments . . .

"The population of this mission consists of:

Married couples, 12 in number,
    from 20 to 50 years of age 24

Widowers and bachelors, from 25 to 40 years of age	8
Boys, from 1 to 10 years, and one girl	20
Total number of persons	52

"This mission was founded with Indians of various tribes, such as the Hierbipiames, Pataguas, Scipxames, Xaranames, Samas, Payatas [Payayas], Yutas, Kiowas, Tovs, and Tamiques. The Samas and Payatas were the principal ones. But all these may be considered as Samas and Payas, whose language is in general use.

"Spanish is now more commonly used, the Indians having married mulattoes and meztizoes, who are called Coyotes in this country.

"It should also be noted that, although this mission was founded in the year 1716 [the year was 1718], most of the Indians in it, and there are more than fifty, are sons of uncivilized tribes; and, further, they were baptized as adults when some were as much as forty years of age." In other words, they were brought to the mission as pagans and converted to Christianity.

Extant census figures show that the population of Mission San Antonio fluctuated considerably during the last decade of its existence: in 1783 the mission had 144 Indians; in 1786, 126; in 1788, 45; in May of 1789, 52 (as above); but in December of the same year, 121; in 1790, 48; and in 1793, 57.

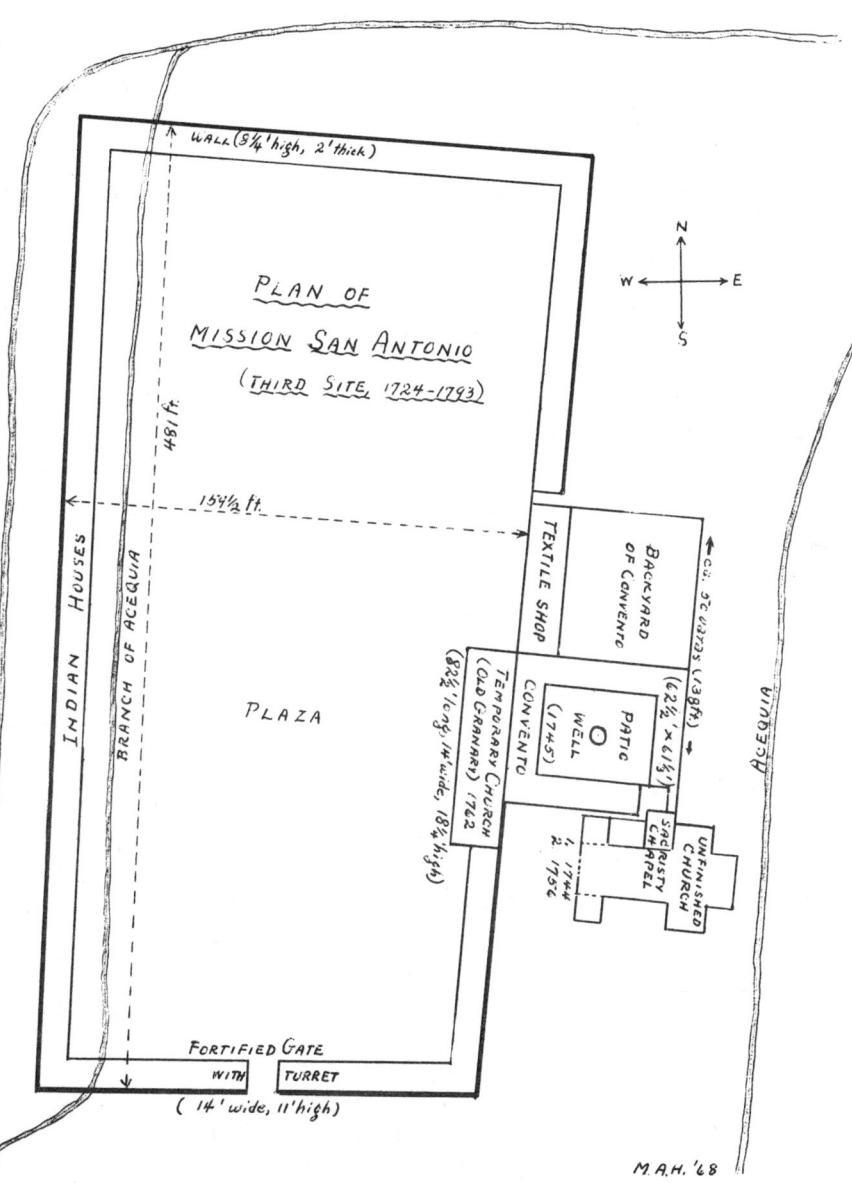

Author's plan of San Antonio de Valero Mission.

Suppression of the Mission, 1793

In 1790, the year after Fr. López made his report, the College of Zacatecas sent its commissary and prefect of missions, Fr. Manuel Silva, to Texas, to see what could be done to improve the missionary situation. Since there were still many unconverted Indians in Texas, he suggested that Mission San Antonio be secularized, that its four neighbors be reduced to two missions, and that new missions be founded elsewhere in the province. The result was that one, and only one, new mission, namely Nuestra Señora del Refugio, was founded in 1793; Mission San Antonio was suppressed the same year; and the other four San Antonio missions were partially secularized the following year.

After the viceroy's decree of January 9, 1793, for the suppression of Mission San Antonio was received, Governor Manuel Múñoz of Texas, who was at La Bahía at the time, issued a proclamation to that effect on February 23; and on April 11, after the governor had arrived in San Antonio, Fr. José Francisco Lozano, who was then the missionary of San Antonio, according to directions received from Fr. President José Francisco López, distributed among 39 mission Indians a supply of corn which was to take care of their needs until the new crop was harvested. This was given to ten heads of families, one of them a widow, and to four other unmarried adults. Each of these fourteen persons also received a pair of oxen, a plow, a harrow, a hoe, and a cow with a calf. Additional corn and other supplies, including ten horses, were given to them two days later.

The other 18 mission Indians who were Lipan Apaches, were to be moved to Mission San José; but they preferred to stay at San Antonio, and were permitted to remain. They, no doubt, also received both supplies and land.

Pedro Huizar surveyed and subdivided the lower mission farm (*Labor de Abajo*); and on April 12, Governor Múñoz gave to each of the fourteen heads of families and unmarried adults a tract of land large enough for the planting of one and three-fifths bushels of seed. A similar plat was given to Pedro Huizar, and another to Vicente Amador, his assistant. Some of San Antonio's cattle, horses, corn, beans, and salt were assigned to the new Mission of Refugio.

Inventory of the Mission

An inventory of the church furnishings was made on April 23 by Governor Múñoz, Fr. President López, and Fr. José Mariano de la Garza, the companion of Fr. Silva. On the 24th the governor also appointed Pedro Huizar and three others to prepare a report on the mission buildings.[30] The latter contains some interesting information about the size of these buildings. We shall translate the *vara* measurement (33 inches) into feet.

The church, still incomplete, was built in the Tuscan style of architecture; it had a transept and a domed roof resting on groups of columns. Its length was 100 *varas* (275 feet), and its width, except at the transept, was 9 *varas* (14.7 feet). One group of columns in the sanctuary had been completed, and three groups were almost completed. The baptistery lacked only the doors. The façade was impressive, having two sculptured statues, one of St. Francis and the other of St. Dominic, standing in their niches. Two other niches were empty.

---

30. For a more detailed account of the inventories made of San Antonio Mission at the time of its secularization in 1793 see Castañeda, *op. cit.*, V, pp. 40-46. A copy of the 1793 Inventory of San Antonio Mission is in RLSJ.

The sacristy, adjoining the church proper on the north side, faced west. It was a large room measuring 12 by 5 by 5 *varas* (33 feet long, 13.7 feet wide, and 13.7 feet high). Though its walls were not plastered, they were neatly whitewashed. It had a vaulted roof, and two doors were set in frames of carved stone.

One of the doors of the sacristy led into another large room on its east side, measuring 8-2/3 by 7-2/3 *varas* (23.8 feet by 21.9 feet). Besides the door connecting it with the sacristy, it had another; and both doors had hooks and eyes. This room had two windows, one facing north and the other west. The roof, consisting of wood and cedar rafters was in need of repair.

Next to the church and sacristy, on the north side, was the friary, a separate building. It was a solidly built stone house, 22-3/4 by 22-1/2 *varas* (62.4 by 61.5 feet, forming a square with a patio in the middle; and in the center of the patio there was a well with an arched stone superstructure and a bucket.

The north and south wings, which were "divided by a hall," and the west wing, which had a corridor, were two stories high. The upper floors of the north and south wings each had five private rooms, and each room was 5 by 4 *varas* (13.7 by 11 feet). But these ten rooms were in need of repair, because the flat roofs were full of holes.

On the first floor of the west wing there were four rooms, larger than the other rooms, an office, and a small room at the bottom of the stairway; upstairs were three private rooms. Here too the roof was partly rotted and in need of repair. Near the entrance of the friary stood a small rampart with a one-pound gun.

Nothing is said of an east wing, but that is where the one-story "dividing" or connecting hall between the north and south wings must have been.

The church and friary were outside and just east of the large walled mission square which was an irregular rectangle.

The wall, on the east and south side, was made of stone, adobe, and mud. The height of these walls was 3 *varas* (8.2 feet), and their thickness was 3/4 of a *vara* (2 feet). The length of the wall on the east side of the rectangle, running north and south was 175 *varas* (480.4 feet). The south wall, running east and west, was 58 *varas* (159.5 feet) long. It was divided into two sections by the main gate, which was 5 *varas* wide and four *varas* high (13.7 by 11 feet). The north wall was half in ruins.

Within the enclosure were the Indian houses, most of which were built against the west wall and faced an archway running along this side. But only 12 of the houses were habitable. The others were in ruins.

On the east side of the rectangular enclosure, forming a part of the wall, stood the granary and just beyond it the friary, the latter being outside the enclosure. The granary was 30 by 5 by 7 *varas* (82.5 feet long, 13.7 feet wide, and 18.4 feet high). Its floor was of adobe. The roof was in poor condition, only the beams being sound.

The mission Indians who had become landowners continued to use the square and to live there. The church and friary with their furnishings were turned over to the pastor of San Fernando. The baptism, marriage, and burial records of the former mission were likewise entrusted to his care. The last pages of the baptismal register of Mission San Antonio, containing entries for the years from 1783 to 1793, must have been lost; for, Sidney Lanier in 1872 found on the last page of this register the following note:

"On the 22nd day of August, 1793, I placed this book of the Records of the pueblo of San Antonio de Valero in the archives of the parish of the town of San Fernando and presidio of San Antonio de Béxar, by order of the most illustrious Señor Dr. Don Andrés de Llanos y Valdez, most worthy bishop of this diocese, dated January 2, of the same year, for the reason that the said pueblo had been aggregated to the parish of

Béxar; and that it may be so known, I sign my name. Fr. José Francisco López, *Parroco.*"

The fact that Fr. López, the president of the Texas missions, added the title of *parroco* to his name indicates that at this time he was temporarily serving as the pastor of the San Fernando parish. Not long after the secularization and suppression of Mission San Antonio, Fr. López was succeeded by a new Fr. President, Fr. José Mariano Cárdenas; and Fr. López returned to Zacatecas, arriving there on August 6, 1794. He died at the College on October 23, 1796.

Subsequent History of the Mission

Mission San Antonio thus ceased to exist after it had been in existence for 75 years, and it was absorbed into the parish of San Fernando. However, in 1801 a new parish was established at the former mission, namely the parish and Pueblo de San Josef y Santiago del Alamo; and its pastor used the church or sacristy of the former mission for divine services from that year until 1825. The members of this parish were the soldiers and families of the Segunda Companía Volante de San Carlos de Parras, a mobile cavalry unit, which established its headquarters on the east bank of the San Antonio River in 1801. They had their own pastor or a substitute until August 22, 1825.

All this we learn from their baptismal register which they brought along from Mexico and continued to use in San Antonio; and hence it has entries from 1788 to 1825. The last entries, those for 1822 to 1825 were made by Fr. José Antonio Díaz de León, the last of the Zacatecan friars in Texas, and by the Military Chaplain of the Presidio of San Antonio de Béxar, Francisco Maynes, who were substituting for the absent pastor of San Fernando. The baptismal register of the Alamo pueblo is in the Archives of San Fernando Cathedral.

It was probably this pueblo that gave the name of El Alamo to the former mission. El Alamo was the name of a town near Parras in Mexico, where the "flying company" had been recruited in 1788. The meaning of Alamo is poplar or cottonwood tree.

The former friary of Mission San Antonio was used as San Antonio's first hospital from 1806 to 1814 and perhaps also after that year. The hospital was founded by Simón Herrera. Dr. Jaime Guerra was in charge in the spring of 1814. At that time he was succeeded by his assistant, Dr. Francisco Favina; and when the latter took sick some months later, it seems that the patients were unofficially attended by Baron de Bastrop. The hospital took care of both soldiers and civilans.

The subsequent history of the Alamo as a fort and as a prison and the stirring story of the siege and battle of the Alamo, February 23 to March 6, 1836, are well known; and it is beyond the scope of this account of the Mission of San Antonio de Valero to relate these events.

In 1841, the Republic of Texas restored the ownership of the old mission to the Catholic Church; but after Texas joined the Union in 1845, the bishop leased the Alamo to the United States Government as a military quartermaster depot. Two years later the Quartermaster Corps capped the façade of the mission church, raised the side and back walls, and built the roof. Thus San Antonio Mission's second stone church was finally completed, but not as a church.

In 1856 the German parish of St. Joseph wanted to make the old mission church its parish church; but at the time there was no other place to which the Army could move, and old St.

Joseph Church was built two blocks south of the Alamo, on or near the second site of the mission.

The United States Army used the Alamo until 1861, when the Confederates took over. After the Civil War the U. S. Army resumed possession until 1876, when the quartermaster depot was moved to the new Fort Sam Houston. The following year Bishop Anthony D. Pellicer sold the mission property, including what was left of the friary, but not the former church and some surrounding land, to a commercial firm for $20,000. The former church was purchased for the same sum in 1883, and placed in the care of the City of San Antonio.

To remove the unsightly business houses adjoining the Alamo church, the Daughters of the Republic of Texas acquired the ownership of some of the former mission property early in the twentieth century; and about the same time, in 1905, the governor of Texas was empowered to do the same. The Daughters of the Republic of Texas sold what they had bought to the State; and the State assigned the custody of the Alamo to the Daughters of the Republic of Texas, who agreed to provide the necessary funds for its maintenance and upkeep. However, in 1909, because of some difficulties which had arisen over the question of what should be restored or torn down, the society asked the State to take charge again, but the care of the Alamo remained in the hands of the society; and in the end, the old friary wall, which some wanted removed, remained standing.

In 1936, on the occasion of the centennial of Texas independence, the Alamo Park and present enclosure of seven or eight acres was made possible by the allocation of funds from the City and the State. The Alamo Museum was built north of the church, so that the latter would have that sense of space and quiet that a church should have; and the Daughters of the Republic of Texas Library, with an adjoining meeting hall, was built on the grounds. The society twice repaired the roof of the church, which was constructed in 1849-1850; and it continues to maintain the Alamo with the loving care that it deserves.

The Alamo is now a worthy and priceless historical monument, honoring the memory, not only of the heroes of 1836, but also of the Franciscan padres who during three quarters of the eighteenth century founded, developed, built, and served Mission San Antonio de Valero.

Legend of the Margil Vine

To the history of San Antonio de Valero Mission, it will not be out of place to add a legend about its early days when Fr. Antonio Margil was staying at the mission (1719-1721). Though his sojourn in San Antonio lasted only a year and a half, Fr. Margil was long remembered and his name was woven into local folklore. At Mission San Antonio de Valero — so the legend relates — there was at this time a little Jarame Indian boy whose name was Shavano. He and his parents had come with Fr. Antonio Olivares from the Jarame Mission of San Francisco Solano in the Valle de San José on the other side of the Rio Grande, when Mission San Antonio was founded in 1718.

Shavano was a bright and precocious lad, not boisterous like the rest of the Indian children at the mission, but frequently given to deep thought and musings. Although he was only five years old, he could speak Spanish quite well besides his native Coahuiltecan dialect. He had learned to recite the Latin Mass prayers distinctly and fluently. He loved to serve Mass for Fr.

Margil, who always offered up the Holy Sacrifice with great devotion. From the great missionary he had learned to love God with all his heart.

Even as a baby at the mission near the Rio Grande, Shavano was a quiet and well-behaved child. For this reason he had been chosen to act the part of the Christ Child lying in the Crib, when the Christmas play *Los Pastores* (the Shepherds) was presented by the mission Indians.

Los Pastores is an allegorical dramatization of the Biblical account of the Birth of Christ in Bethlehem, similar to the medieval mystery or miracle plays. It portrays the message of the angels to the shepherds and the latter's journey to the cave of Bethlehem. Enroute the Devil tries to hinder them in every way he can, while the angels urge them onward. They overcome the wiles of Satan and reach the manger of the Christ Child, and there offer him their homage and love and gifts.

It is a long play. The text, which has been printed in Spanish and in English at San Antonio, consists of thirty-five pages. Its cast of characters includes twenty-four performers. At the present day it is still presented annually in San Antonio, not just once but many times from December 24 to about February 2, and sometimes even up to the feast of St. Joseph on March 19.

According to the legend of the Margil vine, the mission Indians were wont to bring their gifts to the empty Crib in the chapel on the days before Christmas. Little Shavano was distressed because he had nothing worthwhile that he could give to the Infant Jesus.

He was sitting in the lower branches of an *alamo*, a poplar or cottonwood tree, on the banks of the river on the vigil of Christmas, when smiling Fr. Margil — he was always in a cheerful mood — happened to pass by. Looking up, he saw the sad and tearful face of Shavano.

"Come down, my boy, and tell me what is troubling you," said the padre kindly.

"I tried so hard," said Shavano sobbingly, "to find something I could give to the Child Jesus. But I have nothing, nothing at all, except a few colored feathers."

"That's no reason to be unhappy, child. The Infant Jesus came to give himself to you; and he wants you to give him your own heart in return. That is what counts. Any little gift you find will be enough to be a sign of your love. You will see. Do not worry!"

Shavano felt much better now and wiped the tears from his face with the palm of his hand. But he was not quite satisfied. He must find something better to offer than his three colored feathers.

After the padre had gone on, Shavano noticed a tiny plant with bright green leaves sprouting from the ground near the trunk of the *alamo*. His face lit up with joy. Here is something — not much, but something he could take to the Crib in the chapel.

With a stick he carefully dug up the plant with its roots and a handful of ground. He hurried to his mother and obtained from her one of her small earthen jars and potted the plant. Taking this to the chapel, he placed it in a corner beside the Crib.

When it got dark, the presentation of *Los Pastores* was begun at some distance from the mission chapel, and gradually the actors came nearer, accompanied by their audience. When the shepherds reached the entrance to the chapel, they were so astounded at what they saw that they forgot their lines and exclaimed: *"Un milagro! Un milagro!"* "A miracle! A miracle!"

An exuberant vine of rich green leaves and scarlet berries, such as they had never seen before, had entwined itself around and over the Crib, decorating it as nothing else could. Where could it have come from?

Finally little Shavano was able to push his way through the crowd and saw the miracle. It was his own tiny vine which had grown miraculously to become the most beautiful and precious gift of all. Now he understood what Fr. Margil had told him. He knew that the Infant Jesus had accepted his humble gift and was more than pleased with it.

When the Indians learned that Shavano had found the little plant, now suddenly grown into a big and beautiful vine, after Fr. Margil had spoken those consoling words to him, they named it Fr. Margil's Vine.

After the Christmas season, the Indians made cuttings of the vine and planted them beside their huts. All of them developed into luxuriant vines that made their poor abodes look like festive arbors. Since that time Fr. Margil's Vine was found thriving throughout the San Antonio River region.

Such is the legendary story of the origin of Fr. Margil's Vine, as it was handed down from father to son. Whether it rests on some actual occurrence, we do not know. It would not be surprising if it did; for, the life-story of Fr. Margil is full of proved events which cannot be explained in a natural manner.

The fact is that there is a vine in the Southwest that is called Fr. Margil's Vine. It is a member of the Moonseed Family (*Menispermaceae*), otherwise known as the Carolina Snailseed Vine (*Cocculus carolinus* (L.) DC.). In his book on vines, Robert A. Vines offers the following remarks concerning the Margil Vine:

"The genus name, *Cocculus,* refers to the curled, snail-like seed, and the species name, *carolinus,* is the Carolina. The author has been unable to ascertain whether the reference refers to North Carolina or South Carolina, or both. Vernacular names are Coral-bead, Coral-seed, Coral-vine, Moonseed, Red-berry Moonseed, Carolina Moonseed, Red Moonseed, Wild-sarsaparilla, Margil, and Hierba del Ojo.

"This climbing vine could be more extensively cultivated for ornament because of the brilliant red fruit. It is consumed by a number of species of birds. The vine is sometimes mistaken for a kind of Smilax-vine, but most of the species of Smilax have much more leathery and stiff foliage, and thorny stems. The red fruit also distinguishes it from closely related species of the Moonseed Family."[31]

---

31. R. A. Vines, *The Trees, Shrubs, and Woody Vines of the Southwest*, p. 275.

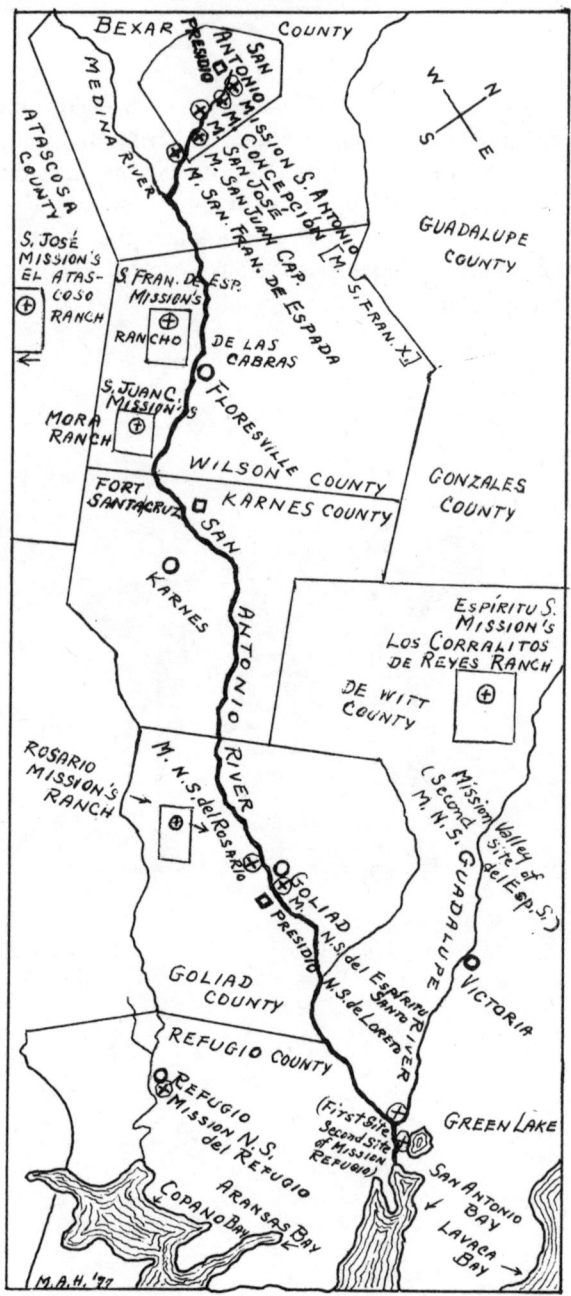

Spanish settlements on the San Antonio River in the late eighteenth century.

MISSIONARIES AT THE SAN ANTONIO MISSION

The list which follows has been compiled from the *Libros de Bautismos,* the Baptismal Registers, of San Antonio Mission, beginning in 1703 with San Francisco Solano Mission, which had three sites in Coahuila, continuing in 1718 with San Antonio de Valero Mission, which had three sites on the San Antonio River, and ending in 1783. The records for the last ten years of San Antonio Mission are missing and seem to have been lost. These *Libros de Bautismos* (the original manuscript copies) are in the Archives of the Cathedral of San Fernando, San Antonio.

The dates given are the years in which the missionaries mentioned made entries in the Baptismal Registers; they do not necessarily indicate the entire period during which the missionaries listed resided and worked at San Antonio Mission.

Thus Fr. Joseph González recorded baptisms administered at San Antonio Mission during the years 1721-1726. We know that subsequently he was in the Coahuila missions of San Juan Bautista on the Rio Grande — this from a letter he wrote to Fr. Miguel Sevillano de Paredes, the Fr. Guardian of the College of Querétaro, on February 10, 1728 (a copy of this letter is in RLSJ).

In a report Fr. Sevillano made in August, the same year, he reported the death of Fr. González: "Murio caminando para los missiones del Rio Grande del Norte." This has been translated: "He perished on the road from Texas to the Rio Grande." It is perhaps more correct to make the translation read: "He died while making a journey [in Coahuila] toward [or for] the missions [of San Juan Bautista] on the Rio Grande." That would not require his return to San Antonio, in 1728, and a journey from San Antonio to San Juan Bautista. The fact is that Fr. González had made a journey from San Juan Bautista Mission to Arroyo Castana in Coahuila early in 1728; and in 1724, returning from Mexico City and traveling from Saltillo to San Juan Bautista, he narrowly escaped with his life when Indians attacked his party and robbed him of his baggage.

1718-1720	Fr. Antonio de San Buenaventura y Olivares Founder of the mission, 1718: Guardian of Querétaro College, 1706-1709; died at the College on June 7, 1722.
1718, 1719, 1727	Fr. Miguel Núñez de Haro (Zacatecas) Back from trip to Trinity River in 1718; refugee from eastern Texas in 1719; missionary of San José, 1720-1755.
1719	Brother Pedro Maleta Companion of Fr. Olivares. He died at the College on June 1, 1737.
1719	Fr. Pedro Múñoz Native of Morelia, Mexico; Indian missionary, over 20 yrs.; president of San Juan Bautista missions; guardian of Querétaro College, 1734-1737; died July 22, 1740, 67 yrs. old.
1719-1720	Fr. Joseph Andrés Rodríguez de Jesús María Assistant of Fr. Olivares.
1719	Fr. Manuel Castellanos Refugee from eastern Texas; died in Texas before Aug., 1728.
1719-1721	Fr. Joseph Guerra (Querétaro) Refugee from eastern Texas; returned there in 1721.
1719	Fr. Agustín Patrón (Zacatecas) Companion of Fr. Margil, 1716; refugee from eastern Texas, 1719; companion of Fr. Núñez at new Mission San José, 1720-1721; founder of Mission N. S. del Espíritu Santo at Lavaca Bay, 1721-1722.

1719-1721	Fr. Antonio Margil (Zacatecas) Apostle of New Spain; guardian of Querétaro College, 1697-1700; guardian of Zacatecas College for three terms, 1707-1713, and 1722-1725; missionary in eastern Texas, 1716-1722, and president of Zacatecan missions of Texas; founded five missions in Texas; died in Mexico City, August 6, 1726, 69 yrs. old.
1719-1724	Fr. Francisco Hidalgo Missionary in eastern Texas, 1691-1693, and 1716-1719; guardian of Querétaro College, 1701-1703; in charge of Mission San Antonio, 1720-1724; died at San Juan Bautista, Nov. 6, 1726, 67 yrs. old.
1721-1726	Fr. Joseph González Assistant and then successor of Fr. Hidalgo; before Aug., 1728, perished while making a journey in Coahuila.
1721, 1749, 1754	Fr. Diego Martín García In 1745 wrote *Breve y Legal Noticia* on missionary methods. Must be distinguished from Fr. Bartolomé García who wrote *Manual para Administrar Sacramentos* in Coahuiltecan, published 1760, used by Texas missionaries.
1725-1726	Fr. Joseph Hurtado de Jesús Maria Subsequently guardian of Querétaro College, 1742-1745.
1726	Fr. Miguel Sevillano de Paredes Guardian of Querétaro College, 1727-1730; then missionary at San Juan Bautista, and president of these missions.
1727-1728	Fr. Benito Sánchez Previously missionary in eastern Texas. Must be distinguished from Fr. Benito de Santa Ana Fernández.
1727	Fr. Francisco Xavier Castellanos A native of Mexico City, and a member of the Franciscan Province of Mexico City be-

	fore he joined the College of Querétaro. Master of novices twice, and guardian after 1748. Died at the College, Feb. 12, 1759, 59 yrs. old. Must be distinguished from Fr. Manuel Castellanos, who died before 1728.
1728-1733	Fr. Juan Salvador de Amaya A member of the Franciscan Province of Jalisco before he joined the Querétaro College. Went to Texas the same year (1728) and remained as a missionary till his death on Nov. 17, 1752.
1729	Fr. Juan Bautista García de Suáres (Resuárez).
1729	Fr. Manuel de Ortúño.
1729	Fr. Nicolás de San Joseph y Sandi.
1730-1733	Fr. Benito de Santa Ana Fernández Missionary of Concepción and president of the Querétaran missions, 1733-1750.
1731	Brother Estevan Zaes Monge.
1731	Brother Francisco Bustamente.
1736	Fr. Francisco Frias.
1738	Fr. Joseph Guadalupe Ramírez Prado Born in the Mission of Las Palmas, Sierra Gorda, Mexico. Was member of Franciscan Province of Michoacán, and taught philosophy 3 yrs. and Canon Law 6 yrs. before joining Querétaro College. Wrote several learned unpublished books. Missionary in Texas for 27 yrs. Died at the College, Aug. 19, 1777, 72 yrs. old. Must be distinguished from Fr. Pedro Ramírez de Arellano of the Zacatecas College, the builder of present (restored) church of Mission San José.
1736-(1763)	Fr. Mariano Francisco de los Dolores y Viana Outstanding and long-time missionary of San Antonio. President of Querétaran missions, 1750-1763. Played important role in establishment of Apache missions in Texas.

1750	Fr. Juan Domingo de Arricivita Author of the continuation of Fr. Espinosa's *Cronica*, published Mexico City, 1792.
1755	Fr. Benito Varela.
1755	Fr. Miguel Aranda Previously missionary at Mission Concepción.
1756-1764	Fr. Joseph López Was at Concepción Mission in 1757. Served as president for a while. Missionary in Texas for 15 yrs. Died at the College, Nov. 22, 1788, 89 yrs. old.
1766-1769	Fr. Joseph Zarate.
1769	Fr. Asisclos Valverde Came from Spain and joined Querétaro College in 1743. Served as councillor, master of novices, and vicar of the College. Missionary for many yrs. President for a time. Died Dec. 3, 1775, 60 yrs. old.
1770	Fr. Andrés de Santesteban At Mission Concepción, 1768-1770.
1771	Fr. Thomas Antonio Arcayos At Mission San Francisco de Espada in 1762.
1772	Fr. Francisco Dura At Mission Concepción, 1771-1772.
1772-1773	Fr. Manuel Carrasco.
1773-1777	Fr. Joseph Francisco Mariano de la Garza (Zacatecas) From San Antonio, went to the Bucareli settlement in 1778, and helped found Nacogdoches at former Guadalupe Mission in eastern Texas, Feb. 1779. President of Texas missions and missionary of San José, 1782-1783. Returned to Texas, 1790, as companion of Fr. Silva, and went back to Zacatecas in 1793. Died on August 15, 1807.

1777-1783	Fr. José María Salas de Santa Gertrudis (Zacatecas) Missionary at San José, 1783-1790. Died there June 17, 1790, and was buried the same day in the sanctuary of the church.
1783-(1793)	Fr. José Francisco López (Zacatecas) Missionary at Concepción, 1773-1783. President of the Texas missions, 1785-1793. Must be distinguished from Querétaran Fr. Joseph López, above.
(1793)	Fr. José Francisco Lozano (Zacatecas) Assistant of Fr. López at the time of the suppression of Mission San Antonio de Valero.

Note: In the Archives of the Cathedral of San Fernando there is also a Baptismal Register for the former San Antonio Mission during the years when it was used as the parish church of the Flying Squadron stationed on the east side of the San Antonio River. It begins in 1788, when the Flying Squadron was still in Mexico, and continues until August 22, 1825. In Mexico the Flying Squadron was known as *Segunda Compania Volante de San Carlos de Parras* (*cita en el Pueblo del Alamo*). In San Antonio its soldiers and their families made up the *Pueblo de San Josef y Santiago del Alamo* (at the former San Antonio Mission). The pastor of this parish from 1822 to 1823 was Bachiller Don Manuel Saenz de Juangorena; but entries 134 to 140, from March to November, 1822, were made by the Franciscan missionary Fr. José Antonio Díaz de León, who also had charge of the four remaining Indian missions just before their final secularization. From 1823 to 1825 the baptisms of the Alamo Pueblo and Parish (nos. 141-143) were recorded by Bachiller Francisco Maynes who was serving the San Fernando church and parish.

The original oil paintings of the five San Antonio missions, made by Theodore Gentilz about 1847, are in the DRT Library at the Alamo. They are reproduced on pages 51-54 with permission. For a short biographical sketch of the artist see Walter Prescott Webb, ed., *The Handbook of Texas*, 2 vols. (Austin, 1952), I, 679.

IMPORTANT DATES

1718, May 1: Mission San Antonio de Valero was founded on the west bank of the San Antonio River.

1719, June: The mission was moved to its second site on the east bank of the river, near present old St. Joseph Church.

1721, Apr. 4: Aguayo's army arrived at San Antonio de Béxar. Chief Rodríguez served as its guide to eastern Texas.

1722, Mar. 12: Returning from, eastern Texas, Aguayo founded Mission San Francisco Xavier de Nájera as a sub mission of San Antonio de Valero, between it and San José.

1724: Mission San Antonio moved to its third site, the present Alamo Plaza.

1725: Aguayo offered to supply all that was needed for the establishment of Mission San Francisco Xavier.

1726, Jan.: Chief Rodríguez told Fr. President Sevillano that he and his few remaining followers preferred to join the Indians at San Antonio de Valero. Thus the new mission was merged with San Antonio.

1731, Mar. 5: Concepción Mission was transferred from eastern Texas to the San Antonio River and established at or near the site of the short-lived San Francisco de Nájera.

1744, May 8: First stones were laid for the first stone church, which collapsed before 1756.

1745, June 30: The mission Indians of San Antonio de Valero saved the villa and presidio of Béxar from attacking Apaches.

Façade of the Alamo (the church of San Antonio Mission).

1756: The second stone church, the present Alamo, was begun at Mission San Antonio, but never completed during mission days. At the mission were 328 Indians, the largest recorded number.

1773: The Querétaran missionaries leave Texas, and San Antonio becomes a Zacatecan mission.

1793, April 12: Mission San Antonio is completely secularized and suppressed.

1801: The Second Flying Company of San Carlos de Parras is stationed at the former mission, and it becomes the Pueblo de San José y Santiago del Alamo.

1806-1814: The convento of the former mission is used as a hospital.

1836, Mar. 6: The fall of the Alamo.

1850: The Quartermaster Corps of the U.S. Army completes the building of the stone church of the former mission and uses it as a warehouse.

1905: The Daughters of the Republic of Texas assume the care of the Alamo as a Texas State Park or Historic Site.

RLSJ PUBLICATIONS

The Old Spanish Missions Historical Research Library, Inc., at San José Mission, P.O. Box 14473, San Antonio, Texas 78214 (abbreviated RLSJ) is a non-profit organization which has for its purpose:

(1) the assembling of microfilm and/or other copies of all published manuscripts and other primary source material concerning the Spanish missions which were established and maintained within the boundaries of the present state of Texas;

(2) the translation of these documents from the Spanish into English, and the writing of the history of the missions;

(3) the publication of these documents and histories.

The Zacatecan Missionaries of Texas, 1716-1834: Excerpts from the Libros de los Decretos of the Missionary College of Zacatecas, 1707-1828, translated by B. Leutenegger, and a *A Biographical Dictionary,* by M. A. Habig. Texas Historical Survey Committee, Austin, 1973. $5.00

The Tarnished Halo: The Story of Padre Francisco Hidalgo, by R. F. Carter, with an Appendix of Letters of Fr. Hidalgo, translated by B. Leutenegger and edited by M. A. Habig. Franciscan Herald Press, Chicago 60609, 1973. $4.95

San Antonio's Mission San José: State and National Historic Site, 1720-1968, by Fr. Marion A. Habig O.F.M. The Naylor Company, San Antonio, and Franciscan Herald Press, Chicago 60609, 1968. $7.50

ions: A History of San Antonio's Five ... *ion* A. Habig. Franciscan Herald Press, ... Revised Bicentennial Edition (paper-

Nothing Itself: Selected Writings of Ven. Fr. Antonio Margil, 1690-1724, Collected and translated by Benedict Leutenegger O.F.M., Edited and annotated by Marion A. Habig O.F.M. 422 pages, large size (5¾ x 8¾), 5 maps, 30 illustrations, Bibliography, Index. $8.95

Guidelines for a Texas Mission: Instrucción para el Ministro de la Misión de la Purísima Concepción de la Provincia de Texas. Documentary Series No. 1. Spanish text and English translation, by B. Leutenegger. RLSJ, San José Mission, San Antonio, Texas, 1976. $3.50

The Management of the Missions. Documentary Series No. 2. The Problem of the Temporalities of the Missions. Spanish text and English translation by B. Leutenegger. Introduction and Notes by M. A. Habig. RLSJ, San José Mission, San Antonio, Texas, 1977. $3.50

Journal of a Texas Missionary, 1767-1804 — Documentary Series No. 3. In press. The *Diario Historico* of Fr. Cosme Lozano Narvais, pen name of Fr. Mariano Antonio de Vasconcelos. Spanish text and English translation by B. Leutenegger. Introduction by M. A. Habig. RLSJ, San José Mission, San Antonio, Texas, 1977. $3.50